BOOK IX

DECODING EXTRA-TERRESTRIAL INTELLIGENCE

METAPHYSICAL INTERPRETATION

O.M. KELLY

COPYRIGHT

Copyright © 2023 Margret Ann Kelly/O.M. Kelly
Series: Book IX (Revised)
First Published as Book IX in "Decoding the Mind of God",
Margret Ann Kelly/O.M. Kelly, Copyright © 2011.

All rights reserved. This book may not be reproduced, wholly or in part, or transmitted in any form whatsoever without written permission from the author, O.M. Kelly, www.elanea.com.

The author of this book does not dispense medical advice or prescribe the use of any technique as a form of treatment for physical, emotional, or medical problems without the advice of a physician, either directly or indirectly. The intent of the author is only to offer information of a general nature to help you in your quest for emotional and spiritual well-being. In the event you use any of the information in this book for yourself, which is your constitutional right, the author assumes no responsibility for your actions.
Book ISBN: 978-0-6458487-9-3

AUTHOR

Author O. M. Kelly, known as Omni to her clients and students is an accomplished author and international lecturer, on Metaphysics, Philosophy and understanding the Collective Consciousness. Omni consults for Member States of the European Commission as a Conciliation Advisor and Rhetoric Counsellor for other International Companies throughout Europe. Omni now resides on Australia's beautiful Gold Coast, writing books, and works as a Life Mentor and Business Coach.

Omni has dedicated her life to decoding the mysteries of the universe. With a deep knowledge of the biblical agenda, mythologies including ancient Egyptology, Asian principles, and metaphysical insights, Omni has discovered the secret that all stories share a coded hidden metaphysical language. Her seminal work, "Decoding the Mind of God", is a compilation of nine volumes of metaphysical information based on the research into the coded information of the Laws of the Universe, also known as the Collective Consciousness, and represents a groundbreaking contribution to our understanding of the metaphysical universe. Now, all nine volumes are being released as separate, revised books, each offering a unique perspective on the universe's workings. Omni's work has been widely acclaimed for its depth of insight, and her contributions to the field of metaphysics have been groundbreaking.

THIS BOOK

Are you ready to embark on a journey of self-discovery? Look no further than O.M. Kelly's groundbreaking book, "Extra-Terrestrial Intelligence". Through metaphysical interpretation, O.M. Kelly (Omni), has unlocked the secrets of the universe and revealed that the key to our next step in human evolution lies within ourselves. This book will show you how to tap into the indelible imprint of holographic importance that is seeded within every human, and unleash the Extra-Terrestrial Intelligence that resides within you. Omni shares her own personal journey of encountering Beings of Light and how it has transformed her understanding of the universe and humanity's place within it.

Omni presents the concept that we all have Extra-Terrestrial Intelligence, and have the ability to tap into the vast knowledge and secrets of the universe. The ancient civilizations left behind clues and teachings about this metaphysical existence and it is up to us to continue to uncover and advance the way we think. Through this journey of life, we can unlock the secrets of our own consciousness and tap into the full potential of our existence. This is a fascinating exploration of the mysteries of the universe and the potential for our own personal evolution.

Readers who are interested in self-transformation through universal truths, Metaphysical exploration for personal growth and a journey of self-discovery would be interested in reading this insightful book on contact with Beings of Light and Extra-terrestrial Intelligence, exploring ancient civilizations and the knowledge they possessed about the universe and the human mind.

CONTENT

Introduction

Chapter One
The World of Extra-Terrestrial Intelligence   Page 1

Chapter Two
The Mind Of The Ancient Telepathic Inheritance   Page 4

Chapter Three
The Extra-Terrestrial Is Your Next Realm Of Self   Page 6

Chapter Four
Energetic Fields Of The Collective Consciousness   Page 10

Chapter Five
You Become Your Own Laws Of Attraction   Page 13

Chapter Six
It Takes One Step To Step Out From The Crowd   Page 18

Chapter Seven
In This Cycle Of Time   Page 21

Chapter Eight
There Is Only One Story   Page 23

Chapter Nine
The Mayan Oracle   Page 26

Chapter Ten
The Doorway Of Time   Page 31

Chapter Eleven
Every Thought We Think Is Measured   Page 37

Chapter Twelve
Knowing Of The Temple Mind   Page 39

Chapter Thirteen
The Forbidden City   Page 42

Chapter Fourteen
The Master Gardener Chen   Page 46

Chapter Fifteen
The Mayan Principles   Page 50

Chapter Sixteen
Contact With Extra-Terrestrial Intelligence — Page 53

Chapter Seventeen
The Teachers — Page 62

Chapter Eighteen
The "Echo-Inside-Essence" — Page 69

Chapter Nineteen
An Attaché Case — Page 75

Chapter Twenty
The Philosopher's Stone — Page 79

Chapter Twenty One
Eleventh Dimensional Lessons — Page 87

Chapter Twenty Two
God Consciousness — Page 92

Chapter Twenty Three
Initial Contact — Page 97

Chapter Twenty Four
The Language Of Divination — Page 99

Chapter Twenty Five
Pneumatic Waves Of Consciousness — Page 107

Chapter Twenty Six
The Worlds Of Holographic Imprint — Page 111

Chapter Twenty Seven
Releasing The Divinity Within You — Page 119

Chapter Twenty Eight
The Five Steps To Birth Your Godhead — Page 123

Chapter Twenty Nine
Pharaoh Of Your Own Land — Page 126

Chapter Thirty
The Afterlife — Page 129

Chapter Thirty One
Our Intellectual Light — Page 134

Chapter Thirty Two
The Three Scholars — Page 137

Chapter Thirty Three
The First Four Books Of The New Testament — Page 140

Chapter Thirty Four
Unfolding The Truth — Page 145

Chapter Thirty Five
The Responsibility Of Accepting Our Consequences — Page 148

Chapter Thirty Six
Your Journey Now — Page 151

Chapter Thirty Seven
ET Cells, Spaceships, Glyphs Of Light In The Sky, Star Seed and Indigo Children — Page 155

Appendix A
My Contact with Extra-Terrestrial Intelligence in a condensed version/time sequence with condensed Metaphysical explanations (including Mayan and Egyptian philosophy) — Page 168

Books By O.M. Kelly (Omni) — Page 186

INTRODUCTION

Have you ever wondered about the secrets of the universe and the laws that govern it? Have you ever felt a stirring inside you, a yearning to expand beyond the limits of your physical body and embrace the full extent of your potential?

If so, then prepare yourself for an extraordinary journey. For within the pages of this book lies the key to unlocking the mysteries of Extra-Terrestrial Intelligence – the next realm of self that is waiting to be discovered within you.

In this book, I will take you on a journey of self-discovery and enlightenment. Drawing from my experiences of conducting seminars in nearly 100 countries around the world and amassing thousands of research notes over the last 40 years, I have uncovered the mysteries of the Collective Consciousness and the Universal Language of Extra-Terrestrial Intelligence.

As I recall my experiences and share them with you, my precious reader, I cannot help but feel a sense of fulfillment. For me, writing this book has been like a marvellous bonfire, metaphorically, where millions of words became sparks that lifted up towards the heavens, enlightening those who listened and read.

Join me on this journey of self-discovery and let us together reveal the truth that lies within us all. For as I have come to know, there is a reason for everything, and everything has a reason. Let us uncover the truth that Is out there and see how it reflects your light out into the cosmos, through you understanding the inner you.

Are you ready? Let's begin. Omni.

The world of Extra-Terrestrial Intelligence reveals an automatic Universal Language that all of humanity is able to realize through its own potentiality. When you understand the commitment of the mathematical codes, the unconscious/higher mind delivers back to you.
Omni

CHAPTER ONE

The World Of Extra-Terrestrial Intelligence

The realm of Extra-Terrestrial Intelligence unveils a Universal Language that humanity can grasp by tapping into their own potential.

Extra-Terrestrial Intelligence is released through the positive actions of our own energy, which creates a reaction through our layers of self-empowerment. As we move forward, our thoughts become more balanced and reliant upon themselves, allowing us to enter into an Extra-Terrestrial alignment of intellect. This alignment reveals our levels of light, which are stimulated through our emotional intellect and thought forms.

My own initial contact with Extra-Terrestrial Intelligence (ETI), was in 1977 – on 11 November, to be exact – when they arrived on my property in Australia that evening. My journey in life since that time has been transformational in understanding the universe, humanity's place within it, through understanding the Collective Consciousness.

I am here to remind you that these pages that I have explained to you are also embedded in you. It is up to you how you relate to my information. We each have our own set of values about who we think we are and what we would all like to achieve for ourselves.

The world of Extra-Terrestrial Intelligence reveals an automatic Universal Language that all of humanity is able to realize through its own potentiality. When you understand the commitment of the mathematical codes, the unconscious/higher mind delivers back to you; in time, this realigns with your intelligence through the Collective Consciousness, which is the Laws of the Universe. Nothing is unexplainable; there is an answer to every question that we are capable of asking. The truth is out there, and that same truth is also a mirror image of the inner you. Please enjoy the following pages, as I continue to reveal my truth to you as to how I understood these sacred vows of time. Keep a dictionary beside you if you are in doubt of pronunciation, as sometimes my words meld with one another, which will open up the blueprint of your DNA.

The journey of our evolution came through the form of cellular recognition; as each species developed, it began to communicate its energetic inheritance through to the other species. These species then formed tribes of self- awareness, and they began to collect their group energy. We, the future of that inheritance, can begin to notice the spectrum that they have earned through their self-importance.

It is the same story with those of us who have stepped up into this "New Age of Contentment, now relabelled as Consentment". While some are busy comforting themselves by staying with the group energy, others have earned a learned desire to release themselves from the fear that has held them back for most of their lives. With newly found confidence, they released their courage to jump up into their next education which released from their cells towards their next evolution. This process is the next step of the whole of humanity's intelligence, yet some automatically place a label on us for something that they cannot fully understand or accept – or that they refuse to acknowledge – in regard to their own inner strength.

It is a natural cohabitation of same-mind energies, climactically reaching up towards the heavens through a desire to reveal their own truth. It is where we feel safe from harm. Remember, though, that we gave ourselves permission to accept the consequences of this highly informative intelligence.

The "New Age" is not new; it has been here for thousands of years. It is the story of humanity's capability of reaching up for the next age of intellectual awareness, which is a timeless story; although, the way in which this story was first understood is what some people only think is new! It is the story of our intelligence coming together as a whole to earn its next step. It is the evolution of the Collective Consciousness evolving itself. A certain percentage of people automatically ascend into this vibration of human consciousness through every generation – therefore, in order for the intellectual equation to be modified, this must be so.

There is nothing new on this planet; it is the same story repeating itself until humanity as a whole understands what has, is, and will become. These are the Metaphysical codes that are written on the walls of the temples of Egypt. These are the Metaphysical verses in the Holy Bible, which are exactly the same codes that led to the development of the Holy Books of the ancient Greek, Arabic and Indo-Asian cultures. All of them explain exactly the same story, which, when we understand it all, is the bibliography – or inner library – of your DNA.

The next wave of consciousness is knocking on the door now.

Your Notes:

CHAPTER TWO

The Mind Of The Ancient Telepathic Inheritance

It was when one walked ahead of the group and stood aside through his indifference – or inner difference – that he began to reach up. When he stood alone, his attitude stepped up through change, where his consciousness could reinforce itself. At first, the others ostracized him for his behaviour; this was to his benefit, as he had found a sense of freedom of self-explanation that automatically changed his genetic inheritance.

Over time, his opposite was attracted to him, and he stood with her; later, when the unit became a relationship, they began the next advanced step from the species of same mind. Through the acceptance of each other and not of the group energy, this species had advanced into its new intuition; others came to notice their light of self-assertiveness and wanted to follow them. It is a pre-birthing into the Collective. When man first learned to stand on his own, the Law of Attraction for the self began; this is an ascension process explaining our "intellectual-duality". That same process is happening to you, as you begin to realize and balance your mind through entering into the right hemisphere of the brain.

It is said that we learned to open up the left brain many thousands of years ago. As of 4,000–3,000 years ago, we began the awakening of the right brain, which led us into a closer understanding of our emotional behaviour, through the form of religion; this, in time, brought forth the Age of Christianity. It was an evolutionary step up into the Collective Consciousness – or maybe an easier name for it would be the Global Consciousness. Those people of the past had their own codes of recognition that had been brought forth from their past inheritance. The positive behaviour of that evolution forced them up into the hierarchical Collective Mind, which, in turn, has brought us forward to this point.

The next wave of consciousness is knocking on the door

now, and so we begin again. Over the next 1,000 years, we will learn to bring the two brains together colloquially for an upsurge in connection to our speech; that balanced brain is what I refer to as Extra-Terrestrial Intelligence. It is through the understanding of the unconscious mind, which is also the mind of the Ancient Telepathic Inheritance – the Collective Consciousness, or what we deem to be God – that we will begin to accept the possibilities of our future inheritance. All this energy has released itself into the Collective Consciousness over millions of years, and it will be available to all of us as we unfold our DNA, which is our devoted inheritance. This will become our New Order of our New World. It is only when you have looked into yourself that this can occur to benefit you and the rest of mankind as well.

As the intelligence of man continues to awaken, we begin to reverse our thinking, and then we have the possibility to see inside ourselves. Through understanding this illusion, you can become aware of your cellular inheritance – or the mathematical program that you were born with.

To carry your tribal family law into your next step of humanity's earnings is how and why you have evolved to be here, clearing your past generations' thinking and programming the mind of your future generations. Once we have accepted this program, it is no longer a detriment to your consciousness; the freedom you create in your mind will allow your intelligence to have the ability to evolve even further.

Once we have recognized and solved the tasks that have been given to us by our tribal law, we are free to collect more information to add to the benefits available to us beyond this program. Your prophecy begins to awaken, and the prophetic justice of self-acclaim shines through you for all humanity to view.

Your Notes:

CHAPTER THREE

The Extra-Terrestrial Is Your Next Realm Of Self

Before you began to question yourself, you thought that Aliens were a species to fear. Your fear coagulates and builds on itself, until you come to believe it, and then it becomes a total rejection – this is where we don't want to know about it! This world is the world of the unexplained, and, until you have lived a personal experience, your intelligence has difficulty releasing your truth into the Collective. These are the mathematics of the mind.

Millions of people have had dreams, visions, or experiences with this species of the Collective Consciousness, and so they have a query about what or who they are. I have given thousands of seminars on the subject, where many thousands of people from all lands entered those halls through their own self-acclaim; that is, they had a personal interest. I never sent out one invitation for them to arrive to hear my words! Most of them had seen something; they either had dreams or felt that they been psychically attacked by aliens.

How did they walk through the door? What drew them to take a seat in my seminars? These are the secrets of the Universe that I am explaining to you. Your unconscious mind is your messenger. This is the myth of Hermes, the messenger of the Gods. And now, through my revealing the sacred codes to you, you are aware of where this position is situated in the human brain (which, you will recall in my book "Decoding Thought", we referred to as the ancient city of HE-RAMSES). Your intuition senses your queries, and the message is unconsciously delivered down to you.

I would like to explain to you that those experiences are where the unconscious mind steps in and takes over, in order to show you what your thoughts are creating for you, through your own thinking, which does not feel justified in itself! Through understanding that the depth of your intellect is identical to the outer boundaries of our Universe, you are being shown the opportunity to exemplify your intellect. This is the language of Metaphysics – or, a more detailed explanation, the "matter of physics".

When people think they see an Alien, they do not realize that it is a reflection of their own Higher Self; that is, it is their next intellectual step explaining to them an illusion of what they have the possibility to advance within their own intellect.

Your next dimension of time is waiting in the wings to step forward and initiate you into your next learned wisdom; all of which collects through your own individual state of consciousness opening you up into the next lesson of statehood, which is the banner earned.

If you feel that it was a negative experience, it is all about what you have already created through your fear; thus, it will work against you. Your thinking has searched for something more to promote an enquiring intuition for self, and, when you have reached the summit of your education, you become too afraid to step into the unknown; as a result, your fear steps forward to create its own dilemma, and this you must live with, until you find the strength to trust yourself enough to overcome this situation.

The Extra-Terrestrial is your next realm of self, expanding and releasing its way through your body – all through your knowledge releasing and empowering itself. Those beings that you see in your imagination are your genes being reflected back to you through the language of the Collective Consciousness – you have reached a zenith through an alliance of realizing your truth. Every level that you reach is reflected back to you through your own concordance, and that concordance is the mathematical mind of the Collective Consciousness, which, by now, you know is the unconscious mind. It is your own wisdom expanding as a result of the freedom that you have earned through both the left (conscious) and right (subconscious) hemispheres of your brain.

You will begin to see this energy once you have connected to the three minds – conscious, subconscious, and unconscious – and allowed them to work together. Those three stages of awakening your mind have collectively been explained through the metaphorical language of mythology ("my theology" or "my way of life"), and these transcribed stories explain to you the evolution of those fifty-five thousand myths of the ancient Gods – "EL", "AN", "EA".

In other words, you are entering up into the unconscious mind, which is where you are introduced up into the world of sonic sound, and that sonic sound is an inverted creation of light that commutes its way through the glandular system and gathers up into the neural pathways of your brain.

For those of you who have a love and respect of self – and a belief in the Almighty – this knowledge becomes easier to accept. These worlds awaken when your mind is focused, and when you understand how to know and project yourself. Through the thinking of the left brain, you are under the impression that we are all "Alien" to one another. Through our Soul's experience, we become familiar with this inheritance; this is carried into the right brain, where we can begin to work with one another. Humanity shares the unconscious mind of the planet with one another, through every one of these intellectual ethereal layers.

Thought attracts thought, energy attracts attention, and like attracts like. The Law of Attraction spins its web to help us connect to our intelligence; this is the gift that the consciousness returns to us, and we as individuals have the ability to share that same unconscious mind with ourselves. It is a nice palace to live in, when you become aware that there is nothing that you do not have an answer for!

Extra-Terrestrials are holographic illusions of what we refer to as "time"; these illusions automatically warp and create themselves through the enhancement of your layers of thought; this is measured mathematically inside your auric fields. Those fields of energy co-create their messages, which they deliver in picture form to your conscious mind from your unconscious mind. It is a coordination of positive light that manifests through the unconscious mind releasing itself back to you. We are given the opportunity to expand through exfoliation; we shed our old skin, layer by layer, which allows the cells of our body to regenerate. When all scrubbed up, those cells bring in a new energetic force of life, which will become our future consciousness.

Allow me to return to communicate to you in the first person. Every vision that we see through Extra-Terrestrial contact is a metaphor of one of our thoughts reclaiming a Metaphysical existence. Extra-Terrestrial Intelligence has released through the thoughts of our energy working in a positive action. This creates a reaction through our layers of self-endowment, where our thoughts arch up to release the next step into the Collective Consciousness of self. It is pronouncing to us our levels of light, which are stimulated through our intellect; in other words, they are thought forms. It is our own balanced thinking reliant upon itself, which allows us to enter into an Extra-Terrestrial alignment of intellect.

Do not allow your ego to fear what you have already lived and become! We can all endow ourselves with this form of hierarchical relationship. When explained through the codes, the word hierarchical means, "the higher arcing of our intelligence collecting itself to ascend our life". Each one of you is the hierarchical adversity of humanity, and, when this is understood, you have set the scene to create for yourself the opportunity to become your own spaceship.

The intellect of the spaceship was left for us thousands of years ago, through the Mayan heritage. Further on is a more in-depth explanation of the codes that were scribed onto the lid of Palenque, many years ago. The explanation of the picture on this lid calls you back into the mathematics of the Universal codes.

Your Cosmic force field is your aura. Your aura is autonomically tuned into the energetic highway that has the information of the DNA of the total Collective Energy of the planet embedded into it, and that reflects your thinking back to you through your Cosmic attachment to self. You are the myth of Atlas holding up your own heaven. In other words, your aura is mathematically condensed with the wisdom of the sonic sound, which we refer to as the unconscious mind. Thus, your sonic sound is the energy of what we refer to as God.

CHAPTER FOUR

Energetic Fields Of The Collective Consciousness

On 31 August 1997, Diana Princess of Wales released her Soul and passed over. The shock to humanity's thinking changed the molecular structure of the whole planet; we opened our hearts, through the emotional grief of the Collective that we all felt within, in regard the loss of a young woman who was so popular in our hearts and minds. These fields stayed open as we waited for the funeral of Diana; more than two billion people from around the world watched the ceremony on TV, all at the same time.

Through the emotional support that humanity shared with one another, we gave that wonderful woman, Mother Teresa, the opportunity to release herself to God. She passed over five days later, still during the gathering of the codes – through the mathematical procedure of seven days – after our hearts had opened for Diana. Mother Teresa's energy was so highly infused into the Divine Energy that she could not die of her own accord; through her having no family to inherit her intellect, she had to earn the freedom for her Soul to relinquish itself to return home. One tall mast opened the door for the other to enter!

Do you remember reading about these codes in "Decoding Death"? She did not have the opportunity to pass her genetic inheritance on to her next generation. The Princess of Wales was buried on the day following Mother Teresa's death. The change of the energetic fields of the Collective Consciousness opened up millions of doorways to advance humanity into releasing their inner feelings. Why? This was through humanity being so emotionally touched, which allowed the Collective Energy to spiral up to be absorbed into the Collective Inheritance of the Consciousness. The funeral service for Diana was held on 6 September, one day after the passing of Mother Teresa, and was in its correct order for the energy of the Collective Consciousness to inherit itself. Our emotional energy morphs throughout the planet, and we are brought back to our own attention as part of the Collective, in order to rebalance the future inheritance of the planet as a whole. Therefore, we must face up to the responsibilities that we have forced ourselves to overlook. This is God, or as I now refer to it as – the Greatest Oracle of the Divine - as well as the Universal Laws, working as one.

Through our allotted time, this awakening automatically happens twice a year. In March through to April – it is known as the "Ides of March" through the interpretation of the Greek and Roman myths, and it was known as a day of infamy because of the assassination of Julius Caesar – one must turn around and face up to the responsibility of oneself! Again it occurs in mid-August through to September, when it is known as the "Winds of Change". Through the Laws of Shamanism, we refer to both of these stages as the "Turning Point". God gives every human the opportunity to turn and face themselves; once after our summer months, and once after the winter. It is where God augurs the repatriation benefits for all of us to review. Those of us who have completed the journey and now live up in the unconscious mind of the Universe are automatically prepared for what is about to happen. We are forewarned, right down to the number of victims who willingly sacrifice their intellect in order for us to change our own way of thinking. It takes a catastrophe to still one's mind. It is through the build- up of the creation of the thoughts of your land, or language, that you are given the results of your actions.

We humans also create the catastrophic weather patterns through the same equation. We earn the cyclones or hurricanes, the volcanic eruptions and tsunamis, through our own eclectic behaviour. We, as the last species to evolve, are supposed to be the highest energetic level of intelligence, and we have the added responsibility for every other species that has evolved before us, as their energy is how our brain has eclectically designed and created itself.

Thirty years ago when I began to realize the importance of self, through my inner education, I thought about releasing these secrets to you. I wondered what could be the worst-case scenario that I would create for you, and how this information would interfere with your life; I soon realized that this was just my own ego re-creating its fear. "Let me learn more. Teach me to understand all" was my cry to the Laws of the Universe. I have now been weaving a web around the planet explaining this information to those of you with enquiring minds who are willing to search for your answers.

These are the secrets that society keeps from you, and the word society is interpreted as "a gathering of ideas". Well, I am responsible for my own society, and I do not believe that we are here to abort our own future at the expense of someone else's control. I have no one to be silent for, only my supreme self. I am a reflection of my own intellectual light, as well as the genetics of my tribal inheritance and the Collective Inheritance; I realize I have earned the right to freely pass this information on to you.

I have a story to explain that can make your thinking worlds much easier for many of you to understand. I would like my grandchildren to inherit a more- advanced understanding of their DNA – more than I had the opportunity to achieve when I was a child. I would like to see our next generation free of the barriers that we have had placed around ourselves, through the preferential treatment of following along in our parent's footsteps.

While you live in your innocence, you are free to move on; when you cannot find the answer to one of your questions, there is someone out there who can give you their answer, which satisfies you in the moment. Yes, I have been told by many, "You cannot give this information out to people; it will surely be misused!" Now come on! Whose leg are they trying to pull? The more-advanced levels of intellect that live in this world shoulder a greater responsibility, far beyond that kind of nonsense! Their self-worthiness will have the strength to carry the rest of the planet through to the next step of intelligence.

Your Notes:

CHAPTER FIVE

You Become Your Own Laws of Attraction

When you are ready to step up into the relationship of your own unconscious energy, your earnings have mirrored to God. You have become your own Law of Attraction, through the Collective of the Laws of the Universe. When we image our thoughts to face the truth of all, we have the strength to overcome any negative interference, whether it is displayed outside for us or on an inner emotional level.

This is how those still trapped in the lower mind think that they have given themselves a priority right to interfere with the innocent mind. They hide under the layers of the garments we all wear. If the garment we wear has creases, it is only through our thinking becoming warped through what we believe to be our truth. If we could face up to our thoughts and release the truth of the words that we think and speak, we would seal the codes that we are manifesting, and then the rest of humanity would reap the benefits and grow. This is truly the Extra-Terrestrial (above the earth) Intelligence in action! Lower minds cannot interfere with or break down these codes. All those who interfere with other people's lives will learn that their own family and country must pay the price for their behaviour before that energy vibrates through to other lands.

And yet, if we rename a few ideas, I will write the word "war", where we are able to pick up a weapon and eradicate someone else's life – all in the name of freedom! For the sake of one man ruling his land (i.e., Adolf Hitler, Saddam Hussein, etc.), millions of people were destroyed. How many Hitler's have there been? I thought there was only one. We are very quickly lead along by our nose, when we do not know ourselves!

Allow me to bring your attention back to the bombings in London, which occurred in 2005, and introduce you to a classic case of how this energy collects its self. The young men who created this furore, thinking that they were helping and justifying the cause that they believed in, originally came from another land. When the bombings occurred, many people gave their lives in order for us to learn and recognize this code. We grieved, and, through that grieving process of opening our hearts to those who suffered, the mathematics of the planet answered our thoughts and created the event of three trains crashing and derailing in the homeland of those young terrorists. As a result, a total of 108 of their own people sacrificed their lives and died for the outrageous act that those terrorists had committed.

So much so that, for these terrorists' own journey to paradise, they had to make room for 108 more of their own countrymen and women to go along with them! It's interesting to realize that, through the Arabic influence, God has 108 names that are foretold. Thus, we can clearly see that these terrorists' own people opened their hearts for the crime committed, and the mathematics answered back.

We only have to take a look at the country of Iraq in order to see how these codes were collected and are still working. If things just happen in our own backyard, we become alerted to the situation almost immediately; when the catastrophe is in another land, we must be made aware of it, and, that awareness does not necessarily happen quickly (although with instantaneous Internet newscasting, it usually does nowadays!). Regardless, we almost always try to place the blame on someone else. We reap what we sow – that is what we must remember. Here, we see God at work again. It does not matter what race, colour, or creed we have attained, or what language we speak – we all have our own seat of attainment, and we all have equal right to live under the same throne of God. There are enough seats available for every human in the auditorium of the Universe.

The higher the position of intellect we achieve, the more honest and truthful we must be when we answer for ourselves; there is no room for innocence or excuses if you have earned an acquired position of attainment in your mind. This is the value of your life accruing itself; and for the world's nations, this becomes an additional responsibility of the governments of those lands. By viewing each country, we can understand that whatever happens is showing them that their truth must reign supreme. Only when enough people wake up from their sleep – or their innocence – will anyone feel responsible for what is happening in and to their own country. Remember: It is the innocent who suffer! Honesty does pay, you know! I spoke these words to my students at a seminar several years ago, and, the following day, the general public became aware of the collapse of Enron. If you recall, initially, this information was "leaked", but, during the months that followed, the public learned how to understand the codes that had collected mathematically to destroy this realm. The truth always reigns supreme!

Another example comes to our attention as to the end of the First World War in 1918; a few businesses had created huge wealth, at the people's expense, and this engendered in a collapse that occurred through the rest of the population, which created a prohibition against alcohol, and which also allowed the governments to try to control the population. As a result of all this, the stock market collapsed, and the Great Depression began to collect itself in 1929. Shades of the economic news of 2008, hmmm? Those that did it right are still around; those that didn't are not! Again, I am explaining to you how the Laws of the Universe reward us from these catastrophes. To explain further, at this same time, we began to become aware of polio. This dis-ease continued to grow, straight through to the end of the Second World War; at that time, it became an epidemic.

Approximately 30 million people died during the Second World War. How many of you are informed of the millions who inherited polio through the microbial consequences that became detrimental to humanity, through our viral attitude of creating and living these wars? Remember that polio is caused by a virus! If all this is true – and I can assure you that it is the truth – we must ask what we are busily creating for humanity to inherit through our current wars of today. Have you ever realized how many people must die for you? That is to say, have you ever realized how many people must pass over through your accepting your own responsibility? These are the Universal Laws that work with God. Did you know that, in order for every student who enters university to enhance his/her education, two people automatically pass over for the sake of that student's commitment? These students have upgraded their own expectations in order to acquire an exalted state of their own grace. Do we reprimand them? Not on your life!

In my book "Decoding Death" I explain the codes of Death, and you learned how our family reacts to inform us of the indentures we will earn. Are you aware that, for every young man or woman who walks in to sign up to represent his/her government, five people will automatically pass over for the sake of his/her actions? He/she has signed an agreement and delivered these lives to the government. The number five (5) represents "change for freedom". The mathematics of the planet is constantly working on our behalf, every second, twenty- four hours a day.

Oh, and don't forget the example of tithing! Ten per cent of the soldiers sent to the front lines will sacrifice for the rest. If the figures go beyond that percentage, we are sliding downhill, stretching the energy of time, and so it will take us that much longer to repair and heal. Slowly, the conscious thoughts of humanity are changing all by themselves, and fewer young people are standing in line to sign up!

This mathematical equation has been going on since we first learned to stand upright. It explains and mirrors our thoughts back to influence us; but, up until now, only a few have been aware of this information. Ask those who have returned from war zones. When you reach my level of attainment through recognizing the codes of the Collective Inheritance, you will have to answer to all those precious young people who will come to you and ask why they are in the transition of a place that we have named "heaven". Each member of these soldiers' families grieves for those young Souls who never quite fulfilled their reason for being here; and, once again, we are creating another furore for the rest of us to endure!

For each one of you who takes on the responsibility of acknowledging the intelligence of accepting the education of the next evolution so that humanity's awareness can prosper, fifteen people will relinquish their lives. These people will pass over for you – that is, on your behalf, as you have entered up into the royal order of wisdom. These are just a few of the Laws of Shamanic Principles that we all accept when we collect our Office of Atonement.

Have we ever thanked those billions of people who surrendered their lives, through their innocence, in order for us to learn and earn this freedom of information? It is only on special days, when, relying on the Collective's emotions – or "energy in motion" – that we remember to say these words of thanks. After we have done so, the pressure of our guilt eases, and our ego forgets all about it.

The greater the force of our attack on our fellow humans, the greater the force of the attack returned to us by God – from the viruses that we inherit to the seasonal turmoil that we create and then must live with. Can you accept now why a plane falls from the sky, a ship connects with an iceberg, a bridge collapses, or an earthquake begins its vibration and a tsunami collects through its strength? This attitude is one that humanity prefers to overlook. The bigger the make-up, the greater the shake-up. There is never an accident; everything that occurs is always an occidental response delivered to us from the Universal Laws – or God (this Greatest Oracle of the Divine)!

Allow me to explain another Law of the Universe: When we wish to leave our own country, we begin by searching for a more advanced country that complements our new experiential way of thinking. We are reaching up and out to exalt our mind; however, we cannot hold onto the codes of our past, and, at the same time, expect to move forward! If your thinking is not as advanced as the country you wish to migrate to, you must change and alter your ideas. When people apply to another country for immigration or refugee status, they must tune out of the laws of their own country, and, instead, uphold the laws of the new land that they are about to journey into. In such a situation, one's life has the opportunity to advance, not to become a detriment to that welcoming country – and certainly not to be used as an excuse for others.

CHAPTER SIX

It Takes One Step To Step Out From The Crowd

You can understand by now how I had to find my courage to teach the participants of my seminars the truth; those wonderful people also needed to release their own pent-up thoughts. Always remember: When the student is ready, the teacher appears.

The many thousands of students who have attended my seminars over the years came of their own free will; some stayed, while others walked away. Some of the students who left were just not ready to release and rebalance their thinking in order for them to understand the codes that their fear had instilled in them. Others simply knew that they had understood and attained the same measurement, and so they were free to move on. As I watched them mature over time, I thanked them all for attending.

My information is just repeating yesterday's thought; so please explain to me why those thoughts could be tucked away and never repeated? It simply cannot be so! They must be returned to us and repeated, over and over again, until all of humanity understands. To put this another way, if we haven't understood the messages that were given to us thousands of years ago, how can we evolve into our truth and attain the home of humanity? Again, we cannot! We cannot do any of this unless we first liberate ourselves from the fear that our ego hangs onto for its own support. There is nothing new on this planet; everything stays with us until it is understood in its mathematical correctness – that is, where it is coerced naturally through our thinking in order to evolve up into its next level. This is the way of the Universal Law – of the Collective Consciousness and the Extra-Terrestrial Intelligence – and of God mirroring back to us.

It takes a tremendous amount of courage to see this journey of life through, from start to finish! We are tossed around in a stormy ocean for years – without an anchor to hang onto or an Oracle to understand or see into – we simply ride the waves the best we can. God does not calm the seas or let up until we have understood our own self-worth.

My pupils around the globe – including the Adepts whom I assist in attaining their Higher Mind – all receive assistance at the beginning through my responsibility. Once they become aware of their own higher realms of intuition, they do not need any help. As their heavenly intellectual worlds come together through their own self-acclaim, they have earned their own freedom and can teach this never-ending story in their own way. They may explain their journey differently than I explain mine, as they have had to awaken their own tribal law, and our ruling emotions create the differences among the tribes. We all rely on our emotions, as it is their position to create our future through our personalities collecting and coordinating with one another in the given moment; they are always available to us, and, when we need to rely on our inner strength, they stand with us.

I have watched so many wonderful people over the years find and claim their wisdom within themselves, through their own personal torture of facing up to self. They have all received the same education and stories from their past, but their personal religious upbringing has never stepped into the intelligence to interfere with my teachings; in other words, all religions understood exactly what I was talking about. If my students had questions, I answered them. Over time, they learned the strength of God through the recorded experiences of their past.

There is only one God, and it does not matter what name we use to refer to God – whether it be Buddha, Jesus, or Allah – every one of these names come under the supreme reign of God. When I am an invited guest in each country, through my respect, I use the same name for God that they do, in order to encourage peace to reign through the understanding of their ego and emotions. I respect their behaviour, which is no different than mine, and so I have earned their respect. We are all one species, reflecting our emotions to suit ourselves, and, as we do this, those emotions bounce from one to the other throughout the Global Consciousness; this suits the levels of the garment we wear, which represents our supreme intelligence – or Extra-Terrestrial Intelligence.

They listen to my stories, waiting for the understanding to open up from deep within them; I, in turn, learn from their stories. We all help one another. Time is the essence and the healer. The Secret Society is within you. Don't worry about the negative side of this level of intelligence; it cannot come into its own fruition, if you believe in your self! Remember, God cares for and looks after you – especially when you care about yourself.

It takes one step to step out from the crowd – just one step! – but, through that single step, the transformation of the emotional self begins. Through inheriting your own belief in your self, as a result of taking that step, you allow the next person to take the next step – and then a whole series of steps are created for all of humanity.

Let us take a look at those who have made their mark – or step – for us to follow: Copernicus, Plato, Da Vinci, Newton, Einstein, Freud, Jung, and the list goes on and on and on. They stepped into themselves and searched; and then they stepped out from the crowd and up into the higher realm. All this was in order for the rest of humanity to step forward, as these great ones all had accomplished the levels of their Soul's intelligence. We are still using their examples to this day.

Your Notes:

CHAPTER SEVEN

In This Cycle Of Time

Some call being alive in this cycle of time "progress". Well! Let's take a look outside your own front door for a moment and view the gift that we have given to each other for all of humanity to go on with.

Millions of people are starving at this time, so we have earned "no nourishment" for those who are beneath us. Millions out of work, so we have earned "no nurturing" to flow through the communities. The rivers of our emotional life are drying up. HIV/AIDS, cancer, and many other dis-eases are rampant, and the only way that dis-eases can be created in humans is through our inner thoughts – or, more precisely, the respect that we do, or do not, return to our inner thoughts, depending on whether those thoughts are positive or negative. As every dis-ease is created and born in the Universe, God will keep on reimbursing us with an added value to each dis-ease that we inherit. We have not yet run out of names for dis-eases.

I would like to add the following to what I have already written in book III on Dis-ease. HIV/AIDS was manifested through "no loyalty to your Higher Self"; we use sex to condone the overtone of our own quality of life. Remember that this dis-ease was instigated through the Korean War, became rampant after the Vietnam War, and is still climbing. If the truth can be realized, it is simply this: The creation of sex is to realign the self, not to place our control over others. That's a big one to swallow, so please chew it over gently. Every six seconds, another human becomes a victim of this acclaimed dis-ease that we call HIV/AIDS. Devouring our sexual overtone is where we have the opportunity to reclaim the justice of self.

One in three people now inherit the energy of cancer, through emphasizing in our thinking, the emotion of hate. Is that progress? Is this what the Divine kingdom wants us to earn? Through us remaining bound up in our own fear, we are autonomically trying to destroy the higher levels of intelligence that our forefathers and -mothers have already created for us during your lifetime. This is the first evolution of God, which has earned the coded name of "EL", which means "everlasting life". Through the word "sex-u-EL", you begin to understand the surging of your own intelligence moving forward and upward. (More is explained further on.)

Why should we continue hiding behind these codes? We will never find this Hidden God embedded in the cells of every human as long as we continue to busily veil and disguise ourselves. If we can create a better world for all humanity by releasing these secrets that not too many of us understand, so be it! Blame me! We have not advanced too much at all over the last 2,000 years, when we still pick up instruments created by fellow humans for the express purpose of penalizing and destroying one another!

My intention is for all of humanity to benefit during their life's experiences by realizing the importance of these laws, that have been passed on to us through the yearnings of our ancestors.

Your Notes:

CHAPTER EIGHT

There Is Only One Story

I began searching for my own Quest of Life over nearly fifty years ago. It all began through my innocence, as I sought to understand how I could reap my rewards of this intellectual dimension of time, which some said was available to me. As I began to understand the information my teachers were explaining to me, I held onto each word; I could not release my information out to others until I received all the answers regarding the questions that I had asked. In some instances, it took ten years for me to earn the correct answers. Before I would accept those answers to the subject at hand, I also had to research the equation as to how this information had collected in order to complete itself.

My teachers explained to me that, on no account, was I allowed to read any book written by others; I had to learn to read myself from within. Of course this did not go down very well with me at first; I wanted all of it! The only two books I clung to were the King James Version of the Holy Bible and a book written by Louise L. Hay (this was a little blue book that my Swami gave to me because it contained affirmations that help us understand how to heal our body). I devoured the wisdom in both of these books. I have since bought at least a thousand copies of each book, and I give these to give to my students who have bothered to enquire of themselves; reading these books has helped them begin to understand their own "laws of conquest" – that is, the "continuing quest".

In the early '90s, I watched a number of television features regarding Egypt and the Pyramids, and then I tried to buy video copies of them for future reference; they never arrived, and, of course, I wasted my money. It was only as I travelled throughout Egypt later on, reliving the writing on the walls of the temples, that I realized the potentiality these codes still had to explain to us how the power of this Universal Law must be understood mathematically in order to be released. I knew that the Universal Laws had given me a challenge to do something with this information. I had to rely on the memory of what I had earned, which, together with my inner vision, explained the "Secrets of Humanity" to me. I have learned never to ask a second time for what did not appear when I first asked for it. It took years of dedication for me to earn each step of the Quest; if I did not get it right, I had to accept and repeat the same lesson, again and again.

My journey has now completed itself, and so I was given the freedom first to speak my words in the seminars I have given, and then to write these books of my own words; I am also free to read what others have written. My heart fills with love as I read the understandings of others according to their own thoughts. I have not missed out on anything new; I was taught all through the discovery of entering up into my own unconscious mind.

The most wondrous gifts that I have received are through my students, as they have been my literary references. As I spoke these codes to them, they could then explain a story in history that they had learned; my spoken words equated and balanced their worlds, and, in turn, that confirmed mine to me. So, to those of you, whose thoughts they studied, thank you for the information that you have left us to go on with.

No one person can claim anything as his/her own; it is available to all who seek the wisdom from within their self. The beauty of this is that we are all shown how to earn exactly the same story! There is only one story, and there are many others out there vibrating to the same frequency and entering into the same understanding as I am – and when you are ready, as you are, my precious reader.

Our inner language is a menagerie of egotistical and emotional thoughts that we are forever searching for within ourselves – we search for this in order to understand ourselves. "If it happened to them, why not to me?" This is the gift that the ancient ones left for us. I am proud to say that my teachings have always attracted to my seminars those minds of humanity that search for the next step to enhance their own education; they are open to receive the pleasure of understanding and knowing how to accept and release their inner truth, and their openness leads them to seek what my seminars offer.

Let us take a pause for a moment so that you can refresh your mind through what you have understood up to this point. Please drink a glass of water, which will refresh your cells and release the fluidic concentration to bring you back into your alignment.

Your Notes:

CHAPTER NINE

The Mayan Oracle

The next step is to bring to your attention to the codes of the Collective Consciousness in regard to the Mayan Oracle. There is a temple near Mexico that many have called the Hall of Recognition (another reference is the Hall of Abundance). Through the Egyptian principles, this is known as the Akashic Records. It also has many other names through the different levels of languages and lands. That temple holds the codes – or the Akashic Records of the mathematical information of our past evolution. The Akasha ("Ark-Ash-Sha") is explained as the exemplification of the sheik, which, through the sacred coding, is the one who resurrects the self in order to exalt himself up into the inheritance of the higher mind.

Inside that temple and buried at the base of the Pyramid, is the sarcophagus of the supposed sun God, Lord Pacal. Let us pronounce the word Pacal correctly: "Pha-Kha-EL". Symbolically, this word represents the "father of knowledge. "Pha-Kha-EL, through the Sacred Alphabet, interprets as, "through the power of heavenly ascension my knowledge heavenly ascends through everlasting life. This first God "EL", through the records of the myth, is initiated into the Collective Consciousness from birth. This holds the knowledge of the first time, which is referred to, through the Shamanic resonance, as the "God of yearning".

We are also aware that the number 144,000 is of significance in the codes of the mathematics. This same number was embedded into the foreheads of both the Mayan Lord Pacal and the Egyptian King "Tut-ANKH-Amen or as some have written -On-". This realization was easy to understand, through the Metaphysical language, once I had collected the codes and understood the Sacred Numerology.

I was very excited when I started to unravel the codes of the Lid of Palenque (my version of "PHA-EL-ANKH-KEY"), which was placed on the tomb of Lord Pacal in the Temple of Inscriptions – or the Hall of Recognition – where these syllables announce to us the sacredness of how we are interpreting our own vision. If we take this language back into the Arabic notation, we can understand the full story that the hieroglyphs of Egypt are announcing to every one of us. They are explaining the language of the unconscious recognition – of our unconscious/higher mind, which is our Divinity, our - Divine Unity - or our inner divine intellect. Paintings are on the walls in many of the tombs, where we see boats carried along by the High Priests. The number of men supporting the boat informs about the message; regardless, this boat was referred to as the "Bja-Ark"! The Bja is pronounced "Bya" and is sometimes referred to as "the ego asking questions"; the men who supported it are the High Priests, which we know are the glands situated around the throat area. As our intellect opens up, these boats evolve until they become our ship (body) to sail the consciousness. Once we have left our third-dimensional reality, we begin to create our own spaceship. (There is more information explaining how this happened to me as you read on.) In other words, they are delivering to us, in picture form, the story of how we were created from the beginning of time. Also the similarity of their writing is delivered to us in a pictographic system, which is the same principle as the Chinese ideograms. An imagistic symbol creates a sentence or idea, rather than a word or letter; this represents the highest expression we can earn through the unconscious mind, as it is releasing our inner truth. This lid is explaining the neural pathways of the ultimate task that our central nervous system can equate to; all in a sympathetic resonance, which operates through a series of interconnected neurons. All of this is the Spiritual coding – or cording – releasing itself throughout our DNA.

The picture of a Mayan at the controls of a supposed – or metaphorical – spaceship is scribed through the codes. (I explained this to you in my book "Decoding Thought", when I delivered the information about the bat that was placed over their mouths; this is through the alignment of our sphenoid area, in connection to the pituitary gland!) It is an explanation of how our intelligence releases through the autonomic responses; that is, through the energy of how our Soul (unconscious/higher mind) enables us to intellectually move forward. The Mayan "Pha-EL-Ankh-Key" is similar to the

Egyptian King "Tut-Ankh-Amen-or-On"; they both represent the same states of consciousness, which are explained all the way through their emotional hierarchical languages. The Mayans explained through the left hemisphere of the brain, where they are explaining the ego through its own transformational journey, whereas the Egyptians explained their story, through the right hemisphere.

When I received this information, it took time for me to digest the information through understanding and accepting that symbolism is the doorway that creates our reality; everything we walk towards in our future has been repeated every day since human existence began! I had earned and equated myself through the understanding that, as we evolve into our own structure of intelligence, we all symbolically build and collect our "ship of light" – and all of this pertains to the result of our unconscious education. More information will be explained further into the book.

Take note that the great Pyramid in Egypt had four ships buried at each of its corners, which relate to the four directions or Medicine Wheel that we use. Those ships represent the temple of how we earn our freedom to sail into the consciousness. The consciousness represents the worlds of thoughts instilled in our brain. Do you see how Homer explained the journey aboard the ship in the Odyssey? Do you remember what I wrote in the previous pages about the spaceship? Maybe now you can bring together the story of how, once we face our self, the Extra-Terrestrial Intelligence of our mind begins to export itself back through the cellular recognition of our body.

In the late '80s and early '90s, I watched as my own body formed the reconstruction of that ship. It began with a vision of a rowboat coming into the shore through a mist; at the helm, was a big blue bird that I now understand to have represented the Egyptian God P'tah, and, at the rudder, was an old man directing the boat onto the beach.

First, I constructed my small rowboat, which, over time, grew into a magnificent galleon that became an ocean liner. Next began the journey of my body, representing a train, bus, motorbike, car, tractor, etc.; with each one of those evolutions, in turn, representing the energy of my personalities in motion, working with the earth. Originally, the Universe delivered the earth to us as our body, which we could rely on to support us.

I could not make head or tail of this vision for a number of years, as I had to unravel what of the various boats of increasing size could do, as well as how any of it benefited and worked with the creation of progress. Through the laws of Shamanism, I understood that all this was here to serve us, replacing in us what we did not have – and, perhaps still do not have – the inner strength to accomplish. Our inner totem was constructing itself through the evolution of the technology that we have gratefully accomplished and achieved to be of service to the planet at this time.

My last step began with planes – from a little crop duster that removed the irritations of the mind, to a helicopter, an airbus, a jumbo jet, a stealth bomber, a rocket ship, a satellite – and, finally, the space station! My dreams and visions revealed all to me; if I did not understand each individual message, the story had to begin all over again. That is when the creation of the spaceship began; it has taken many years to construct itself, and it is still in the making to this day – I am permanently rewarded as I continue to unravel the codes.

I receive the information in a format that creates a geometric grid, through the delivery of my unconscious mind, and through certain colours vibrating into wave measurements. All of which supports my mind in order for it to gestate and open up into other worlds. My autonomy is registered with this energy throughout the Collective Inheritance forever. Sometimes I battle finding out what has been added for me to endure; as always, it reveals itself at the appropriate moment. As I take another step forward, a new and exciting story begins that just adds to my life.

Each evolution was a story of my emotions conforming to the justice of the higher mind. The outside was mirroring my thoughts inside. I felt these worlds magnetically attracting themselves to my force fields – or my aura – as I went through the myths of the ages. I became aware of "beings of light" transforming their justice with mine; I could read this evolution through my own emotional inheritance, as to what these stories were here for us to produce, in order to release the truth that automatically releases from our own DNA.

Your Notes:

CHAPTER TEN

The Doorway Of Time

The relation-ship that we form with our higher selves is the unfolding of the mathematics ("Ma'at-He-Ma'at-ic's") of the mind, and that was one of the first important awakenings for me. The symbol below represents the diamond that we refer to as the "Doorway of Time". Delivered to us through the Egyptian principles, it is one of the most powerful symbols of all, and it explains how to begin to open the heart. Every language, since time began, also includes this symbol, explaining to us to how we enter up into the angelic form. We have named this symbol Ma'at; the visual representation of Ma'at is a woman with wings.

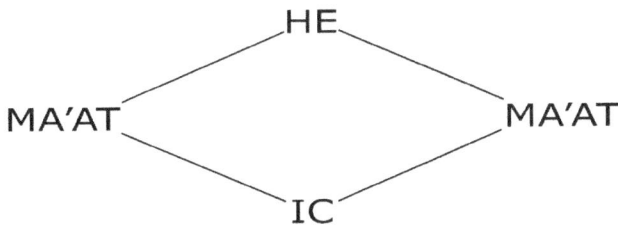

Interesting, isn't it, how the logical word mathematics originally developed through the Collective Consciousness? It is through the DNA releasing its own embedded knowledge as each one of us turns to face our self, which explains the "opening of the heart" ceremony. This is the hieroglyph of the ibis-headed God, known to us as Thoth; he is the one who holds the measuring rod, where he weighs the feather and the heart on the scales of Anubis. Anubis, symbolically, is the one who represents the ancient loyalty of self; he represents the sentinel of the underworld, and the underworld is where we must walk to free the control our ego has over us – and we know, by now, that the ego's control, which is also our fear, represents our past! Anubis is the gatekeeper that stands at the entrance to the doorway as we enter into what most refer to as the "afterlife". No! That is not right! The afterlife is where we enter up into the unconscious mind; it is known as the entrance into the fourth dimension – or the temple area of the Divine kingdom. And that is right here on earth!

Through the mathematics accumulating within our thoughts, we enter into states of enlightenment where all our feelings release through the heart. Once we are through this education, we return our wisdom to be of service to others. Ma'at represents the unfolding of the right brain, which is the internal law of our emotional strength in regard to how we are brought up into our unconscious mind – or how we are being measured unconsciously through the opening of the heart. It is here that we collect our combustible energy and create our sonar devices in order to tune in to the sonic sound of God.

We are now entering into the first step necessary for us to understand the correct meaning of that wonderful word love. That is a huge step forward to know that these two words – mathematics and love – are living adjacent to one another. We are all beginning to birth our angel within. "As we receive, so shall we give."

Our inner angels manifest through the courage and strength that our personalities have earned through accumulating their own respect. In other words, our personalities have learned to master their own Divinity. Through this newly found strength, we release our written words; this is where we always begin our story – through the heart. Do you recall the myths of Mercury with his wings on top of his helmet? Those wings represent the flight of the angelic being – or highest level of attainment to the mind.

The word "HE" tells a wonderful story of the henu bird – or the "B'n B'n" or "Bja-an Bja-an" bird of the Egyptian principles. In the Chinese language, he represents our "heavenly energy", and, its symbolic representation is the crane – or crown bird – that lives on top of the mountains. These birds symbolically represent the highest angelic resonance that we humans have the ability to earn. Each time we venture into a Chinese restaurant, we see pictures of this wonderful bird on the walls. It is the crown bird that transforms into the Golden Phoenix, as explained throughout the Asiatic laws, right down to the children's stories (from the classic books and movies that our children still enjoy today to the newer ones, including Harry

Potter, The Chronicles of Narnia, and many others).

We also have the explanation of the wonderful Archangels that we have named UriEL, GabriEL, MichaEL, and RaphaEL – all of which represent the glands in the neck. In my previous books I have explained, how the end of the earth (decoding of the Egyptian principles) ends in our neck. (Recall my previous explanations regarding the story of Urt, who became the spokesperson and elder of the tribe, as he was the person – personality - first to understand these sacred laws and had earned the right to speak on behalf of the others), as we take our next step into walking through the Egyptian seven bands of peace, or as elucidated in the Book of Revelations – the seven churches of Asia and other myths – ascending into the heavens or the afterlife (above the neck area – head). These glands represent the final steps, of our third dimensional reality, where we arc our entire inner spectrum in order to begin our journey into our sonic sound waves; this is where we find ourselves tapping into the unconscious/higher mind. Once we reach these levels of concordance with God, or the "**G**reatness of the **O**racle of the **D**ivine" we become the "conductor of our own orchestra", as we have earned our freedom to view and create our thoughts for the rest of our life! (More of this ideology is explained in my book "Decoding The Revelations of Saint John The Divine: Understand The Role You Inherit".)

Every myth created is an explanation of our mind delivering back to us an ancient memory of our evolution. Now can you begin to understand and see how the world of symbolism has created our reality?

Allow me to refresh your mind referring to my book "The Alphabet and Numerology", where I explained the evolution of the huge 5.5-metre-high Bodhisattva figure, which is housed in the Temple of the Buddha's Fragrance at the Summer Palace in China. This glorious figure symbolically represents the unfolding and opening of the Soul mind, through the Collective Consciousness; the forty-four arms bear gifts, and the eleven heads represent the eleven strands of wisdom that release from the DNA. Remember that we also had eleven Apostles, once Judas had been exalted up into the Divine Energy. We can see how the eleven strands of our DNA must be supported and balanced by the twelfth strand of emotions, which occurs through the opening of the heart. We can see how, through the education we receive and release mathematically, these eleven strands manifest our inner wisdom. Freedom releases through our mind; and then, with an open heart, we return our teachings back to humanity.

Also being shown to us is how the Chinese brought forth their explanation of the story of Egypt. Remember that the Chinese lived in Egypt and studied the hieroglyphs 1,500 years before Christianity had even emerged (written and explained in other books). The Bodhisattva symbol created the next step; this is where we see how the Chinese interpreted their understanding of the ancient codes, of the same story.

The Egyptians left us the tombs of mummified pharaohs, wrapped in linen cloth, with the tools of trade threaded throughout the layers. Those tools are symbolic and available for us to use for our next experience. The symbol of Ma'at with her wings outstretched and the tools of trade swathed in the robe of the mummies are also identically released through the presence of the open-hearted Bodhisattva, with each arm representing the movement of wings in motion, and with the gifts placed in each hand representing that which we have earned through our positive action.

Again, we note the figures that we have absorbed through the Mesopotamian understanding of the Sumerian philosophy, through the memory of their hieroglyphs explaining to us the worlds of our thoughts; through their winged species explaining the Metaphysical journey of walking through the underworld of the past, to reach and attain a permanent phase of enlightenment. Remember that the birds and animals are different stages of the evolution of the human brain. Their program was explained to us as the left hemisphere – which was known as "Nam Tar", and which was changeable – and the right hemisphere, known as "Nam", which was not changeable.

Some have named this the "Annunaki energy", so let us break this word up and see where it leads us into the Sacred Alphabet. "AN-Nu-AN-Ark-Ki": Annu is still used in many seminary disciplines today, and it is interpreted as "the seed", which represents the germination of the next thought. As it was interpreted in the past, there is another "AN", which represents the educational growth of that seed; and then we bring the last two syllables together to represent "Ark-Ki". As I bring this word together, we receive the explanation of having earned the key, and arching ourselves up into the Divine knowing of our intelligence.

Every relic; still here on the planet explains the entrance up into the Metaphysical existence of humanity's next step; this is where we continue to live our life, therefore, we are then answerable only to the intelligence of the unconscious mind. We read exactly the same stories in the Book of Revelations; millions of us read and speak these words every day. What I am explaining to you is the Shamanic journey, as is it known to us today. You all have the possibilities of entering into these higher definitions of intelligence through finding and releasing your freedom within. You can do this through the vision, or dream worlds explaining your thoughts back to you; through your innocence, you begin to refer to this as your "imagination", which I have renamed "the image inside your nation". Are you beginning to understand these codes that have been repeated throughout the books?

The Mayan people left us the gift of being able to unravel the symbols of their heavenly fields of light. They also tuned in to the Collective Consciousness and brought forth their interpretation of the hierarchical mind, owing to the language of choice at that time. One thing I did become aware of was that the Mayans, and their mathematical understanding, were more accumulative as to explaining the evolution of the left brain, and they turned their education into a game. These High Priests of their time had also earned the understanding of the secrets of the Universe. It all depends on the pronunciation of the language we speak as to what personality steps forward to rule. Their stories have brought through a different personification of human consciousness, and yet, through the mathematical codes, they explain the same story as the Egyptians.

The examples the Mayans left for us are on an outer level,

which explains why the Egyptians have given us the journey on an inner level. Now we can begin to understand the two heads in the base of the Pyramid in the Hall of Recognition: One is dark, the past, and represents the logical left brain, and the other is light and represents the future, our emotional right brain.

The Egyptians left us the understanding of how we bring the functions of the nervous systems through, from the left brain into the right brain, in order to create the emotions of responsibility that one allows one's self to receive. That is also the walk through our personal life that we take to unfold the Hidden God within. It is the pathway used to explain how the Bible was constructed from the past, and these stories were gathered together to begin the worlds of Christianity – or the "Christ (the light) in our unity".

Our journey of humanity over the last 2,000 years has brought us up to this point, and the next step commences as we enquire and ask the Collective to show us our next step. We are now entering into the next phase of the Divine language evolution; this is where we combine both brains into the oneness, which will create huge shifts of intelligence into our consciousness. I look forward to the next 2,000 years.

Your Notes:

CHAPTER ELEVEN

Every Thought We Think Is Measured

Over 3,000 years ago the Chinese lived in Alexandria, Luxor, and many other areas in Egypt. They remained in Egypt for many years, gathering information from the temples and writings. When they returned to China, they took this information with them. China, when interpreted through the codes, means "the energy of 'AN' moving on". As you know by now, "AN" is the second God that we evolve through in order to accept the inner education of how we "ark" our mind deeper into accepting this Covenant we have biblically made with God. Through the Chinese esoteric language, we refer to this area as the "Middle Kingdom".

The Chinese have given us a record of time immemorial through which we can wander in Beijing. This is the Forbidden City (or, as it literally translates from the Chinese, "the Purple Forbidden City"), and it gives us a very interesting story that explains the symbolism of the Chinese interpretation of discovering the Divine mind through the sacred codes. Ordinary minds were forbidden to enter the gates until their intelligence had proven and balanced itself; at that point, they had the opportunity to go on with their education. The colour purple represents the forehead of the mind. It is the screen of the mind, where the internal vision comes through to us from the unconscious mind, which is coded into the Metaphysics of the myth. Some religious orders refer to this area as "the home of Saint Germaine", the Ascended Master who metaphorically represents the doorway of germination of new ideas to heighten the mind. So this whole temple has been constructed to explain the coded mathematics, in regard to their interpretation of the unconscious mind.

The colour purple comes through the production of our Alchemy, and the way in which it releases the inner rainbow that harmonizes through the arcing of our own responsibility of self. Always, the right chemical is created when our thoughts are in perfect harmony with one another. Where is this colour situated in the rainbow we receive after the blessing from

God that is the baptism of rain? As it is out there in the sky, so, too, it is within you.

Every thought we think is measured on our own behalf, through the unconscious mind. This may explain why the country of Germany is known outside its own boundaries as the "Land of the Philosopher", through their understanding of the original language. They have this uncanny desire to trust their intuition, and, over time, their technology has spread completely over the planet! This is all to do with their personalities and how they pronounce their written word; in other words, how they have aligned with their intellectual language.

Your Notes:

CHAPTER TWELVE

Knowing Of The Temple Mind

In 2005, I took a large group of my European students to the land of China, where we anchored into five provinces in search of the original tribes. We found four tribes still connected to their original beginnings, and they all still live in the earlier evolution of their DNA. Having never moved away from the area, they still speak and live in their original state of grace. Although their spoken language is the same as the original, the written word of their language has changed many times, as the autonomic progress of each new generation has changed the old structure; this evolved as each generation birthed up into the higher mind.

Over the last 2,500 years, twenty-four Emperors of Heaven have ruled the land of China – including the more famed dynasties of the Shang, Tang, Han, Ming, and Ch'ing, as well as others. Between them, these emperors' architects and workers built what we know as the Purple Forbidden City, which houses 9,999.5 rooms. At the end of a corridor in the last temple constructed, is a small room with only two of its walls completed; that small room "half a room", or the ".5" of the 9,999.5 rooms. When you step into that small space in this temple, you become the other half of the room – you replace the two missing walls, and so you complete the room when you enter it. I realized that the two missing walls represent the two hemispheres of the brain! Thus, I felt that I had completed the codes of the 10,000 rooms, through the Sacred Numerology. Throughout the teachings of Chinese mythology, we have discovered the 10,000 Buddhas and also 10,000 Eyes of God, explained to us as the tail of the peacock. Each Buddha and room in the temple represents the third eye! We discover something else about the number 9,999.5, as represented in the Chinese temple. Through the Sacred Numerology, 9,999.5 interprets as, "the knowing of the temple mind through the freedom we have earned". The Heavenly (Temporal) Emperor had full and supreme reign over the people at that time.

This story is similar to the Old Testament Sages, all of whom were there to keep the Covenant of God alive. Eleven mythical animal Gods also protect those Chinese temples; thus, if we add the emotions of the Temporal Emperor, we have the sacred number twelve (12).

Or, we can ask, had they also worked out the understanding of the mythical codes to the Apostle Judas Iscariot? Very few understand these codes, even among Adepts of Metaphysics. Christianity's teachings tell of twelve Apostles, one of whom was named Judas Iscariot. This being, was supposedly eradicated from his position as an Apostle through Jesus revealing the secrets to him. In Mark 14:20, Jesus reveals, at the Last Supper, that this was to be his last meal, after which he would be betrayed. This is what Jesus says: "It is one of the twelve that dippeth with me in the dish." Allow me to explain this sentence through the Metaphysical language. The dish or bowl represents the nourishment that one receives, meaning that Jesus was prepared to share his intellectual knowledge with Judas. When the education was finalized between the two of them, they had equalized their energy as one; in other words, they had become one mind. Through Judas acknowledging the mysteries, his name changed from Judas to Ju-dius, from the Latin language of the Romans, where ju means "you", and dius means "to have become a Divine person"; thus, we can interpret Judius as, "through the Divine intelligence, I understand my Soul".

Three days later Jesus surrendered. Through the secrets given to him by Jesus, Judius had evolved beyond the other Apostles, and he relinquished his Apostleship in order to accept his next level of intelligence. As a result, eleven Apostles remained. Now you understand that the way in which you bring the hidden codes together determines how you read the interpretation of these sacred laws.

The Gods – be they Mayan, Arabic, Aboriginal, or Asian – are the propelling emotions of our totem energy; that is, they form the wisdom that we are able to draw from the evolution of the species, which we need to strengthen us when we doubt our own possibilities. When we are devoid of these emotions, the Gods replace in us what we are too afraid to accept about ourselves. This is the strength of the totem energy, which has been mathematically collected through the Universal Laws of God.

Your Notes:

CHAPTER THIRTEEN

The Forbidden City

China's Forbidden City (which, remember, translates from the Chinese as, "the Purple Forbidden City") holds the keys to the kingdoms of the human mind – that is, it explains, symbolically, how our thoughts register and connect with the brain. It is a step-by-step tour of the delivery of the hidden language to every human. The brain functions and works through the language that it receives from the central nervous system, as well as the beat of the heart, and this is then delivered throughout the glandular systems and up into the unconscious collection zone. This unconscious energy is responsible for every thought that we are capable of producing and collecting through the vibrations which create our sound waves. If we care to look through the temples and palaces of today, we will see the symbolism that is still carried out for us – and that will continue until we can learn to unite with the "upper echelons verses or stratum of self", achieving the royal-ness of self! When this royal state is reached, it is depicted by people clothed in white on the temple walls. This symbolism does not signify an afterlife or heaven; rather it symbolizes those who have transcended the limitations of the third-dimensional earthly mind. They have been justified by the laws of consciousness, ascending into an angelic or higher intelligence - our heavenly mind.

In 1974, just outside the city of Xi-An (which, when decoded, explains that one's education has become the completed intelligence of God), an underground pyramid – or vault – was unearthed. So far, more than 8,000 warriors, as well as a myriad of animals, have been discovered in this vault. In other words, it is a replica of the Chinese mathematical understanding of the biblical rendition of the story of Noah's Ark. Artisans are still repairing the broken pieces of the treasure so that the next phase of warriors can emerge. Subsequently, other pyramids and vaults were unearthed. This treasure trove of our ancient past is situated over an area of many kilometres in size, all of which will be unearthed for us to view in the future. Once the restoration has been completed, we will find that the codes equate to a total of 10,000 warriors, as that is the understanding of the sound waves of the Sacred Alphabet and Numerology, which the Chinese language has already earned.

The Emperor in that same area was named Ten Chi Huan, which, when decoded, interprets as, "I am my Soul's energy through the heavenly understanding of my education, as to the oracle of the divine in informing us of the greatness of God". This first pyramid opened to the public explains the biblical rendition of Noah's Ark, where the ship was created, and then the animals were selected to evolve into becoming the human brain. Do you see how the ship has played such an important part in the Extra-Terrestrial Intelligence? In fact, it still does! These warriors represent the personalities that we have available for our use.

Each of these warriors has a different face, as, symbolically, they each are responsible for one of the 10,000 faces of Buddha – or God. Through their mathematical equation, these warriors represent the personalities of the mind. Not a single face repeats; we can see 10,000 distinct expressions. Through my journey to China, I discovered that the sculptors recorded their identities by inscribing the lifelines of their own palms into the palm of each warrior's right hand, which represented the original blueprint of each artist's own DNA. Did they do likewise with the 10,000 unique faces? Is each warrior a reference of self-likeness created by each of these artists and imprinted for posterity on each statue? This wonderful "Eighth Wonder of the World" reminds us, once again, of the journey of the Soul. Are you now beginning to receive a bird's eye view – or an angelic understanding – of how the ego of the planet must be stringently brought back into an order of competency? For, this is the only way that we all will be free to inherit the earth!

Are you beginning to pick up the symbolic references as to how the sacred language communicates back to us? Maybe now I can ask you if you are becoming aware that there is a giant program throughout the Collective Consciousness that every human must adhere to. You cannot realize your own ability to change your individual program until you have found and contacted your inner self!

The Chinese Temple of Death houses the 10,000 Buddhas that represent the personalities of self. In ancient times, these personalities were referred to as the Hidden Gods within. And remember that these Gods were those personalities that became confident in themselves, which, in turn, brought forth your inner strength! In many Asian countries, those Gods are referred to as the "Nagels" (similar sounding to the word nails) In both the old Arabic language and also the German language, the word nagel means "nails". And what do nails do? They reinforce, strengthen and hold the pieces together. In China and in the Arabic countries, the doors of the temples must have eighty-one nails embedded into them. The sacred equation for this is: $9 \times 9 = 81$. These nails symbolically serve as a form of protection for those who enter into the temples. These people are fully protected from any negative vibrations and, until each initiate had passed each level, he/she could not venture through or up into the next doorway of wisdom.

Nails are also the protectors of our fingers and toes, which represent our understanding and our action. Our nails are created through the residue of our bone marrow. Our bone marrow is the biblical rendition of the written word; it is the creation of our inherited intelligence, which has been collected through the thoughts of our past generations. Remember the explanation of the Egyptian story of the Bja? The Holy Bible explains this same vibration, in the Book of Revelations, which describes the 144,000 people – or personalities (aspects of self) that we are born with – who will be saved. All of this knowledge explains the results of the twelve tribes of Israel releasing their positive self. And remember that the word Israel explains our entrance into the Divine language of our unconscious mind.

Do you sense the similarities in the stories that the ancient ones left for us? Are you feeling more informed in regards to the relationship to your self now? Hopefully so – at least a bit more than when you began reading the books in through my set of Decoding who you are! You can become every inch of creation, once you accept that every myth is the story of each individual being. I can take you higher and higher explaining these mathematical codes of the Collective Consciousness, but I do not want to lose you along the way. All I ask is that you accept the evolution of your self, through you hearing my words, as spoken through my truth as I have earned it. Remember, hearing is accepting on an inner level, as you are looking through each word, and, therefore, understanding and accepting each word; whereas listening is becoming aware, and so is looking at, not through, each word!

Do you sense the similarities in the stories that the ancient ones left for us? Are you feeling a deeper understanding of your relationship to your self now? Hopefully so – at least a bit more than when you began reading my books. You can become every inch of creation, once you accept that every myth is the story of each individual being. I can take you higher and higher explaining these mathematical codes of the Collective Consciousness, but I do not want to lose you along the way. All I ask is that you accept the evolution of your self, through you hearing my words, as spoken through my truth as I have earned it. Remember, hearing is accepting on an inner level, as you are looking through each word, and, therefore, understanding and accepting each word; whereas listening is becoming aware, and so is looking at, not through, each word!

Encrypted throughout the codes of Sacred Numerology, the number 10,000 explains a story to us: "I am my temple Soul", it proclaims – or, it reveals that we acknowledge: "I am my Soul and my Soul mind". The first explanation is for the left brain; the second is for the right brain, which brings the responsibility of our thinking totally back into ourselves. No one else is responsible for our thoughts, so we must all learn to uphold our own Law of Balance and Harmony.

Your Notes:

CHAPTER FOURTEEN

The Master Gardener and Chen

I would like to share another story with you; this is about a day in China that I will never forget. While walking through the avenues of the bonsai gardens with my guide, Chen, I had the pleasure of meeting the master gardener. (It is interesting to note that the Chinese, like the Aborigines, address you by your surname. Why is this so? Both cultures have already evolved up into the Divine language of the unconscious mind!).

Back to the story! This master gardener had been working as a caretaker in these same gardens for more than ninety years. He began his apprenticeship at four years of age. In all of those years, he had never taken a day off from his work; he explained to me that he had a responsibility to his "children" – which were these magnificent trees – as they were beings lesser than he, and so he must nurture them so that they could find their own strength. He taught them how to talk to him, and he encouraged the stimulation of their mind, through tipping and pruning their branches twice a year – once in the spring to prepare them for the summer, and once in autumn to help them prepare for the winter, as this stimulated and educated their life force. Remember the turning point that I previously spoke in other works in regard to humanity; for, we must also turn and face ourselves at these same times each year.

It took a period of twenty-eight years for this master gardener to finalize his apprenticeship (the equation for this is 4 x 7 = 28), after which time, he could take full responsibility for his work and not have to rely on others' judgement. His training was the same as his own master's had been. He had promised the trees that he would be there for them, that he would talk with them and share their responsibilities. Some of these trees were many hundreds of years old, and yet they still survived in these small clay bowls.

As I looked into his magnificent eyes, he related his stories to me, all the while gently touching the old tree that he was working with. This tree was the oldest in the gardens; it had only the shell of its trunk remaining, with one small branch that had five leaves poking out at the top. According to its chart, this tree was around 1,100 years old. My heart shattered into a thousand pieces at the love that poured from him as he spoke his words. His own family had come and gone, and he was all that was left, so now he could devote the rest of his life to attending to his Spiritual family. My goodness! I could see how his strength had released through his power coming together in order for him to achieve his self-acclaim.

I did not want to walk away and leave this beautiful man; I realized that I was in the presence of wisdom. As I bowed to him and brought my hands together, I blessed him and thanked him for his time.

Chen and I walked away, and, as I dried the tears from my eyes, I felt ever so humble. Chen's arm slipped through mine, as I was teetering along the path, and he said, "Let's go on to the teahouse and have a small pause." As we walked along, I listened to Chen humming to himself, and I noticed that he would repeat the same sound over and over again. I asked if the song was an old one, and he smiled at me, saying, "No, it is not. It is I, calling myself back into harmony. Some of my 10,000 personalities need attention, but they are of no consequence in this moment, so I am informing them that we will share with one another at a later time.". My heart melted when I heard his words. How precious to be able to communicate so honestly with the self! What an easy way to be in control, to de-stress, and to release the pressure of the mind – all at the same time! it is so simple, isn't it? We Westerners still have such a long road to travel!

***

The last Chinese empire, the Ch'ing Dynasty, came to an end in 1911, with the Empress Dowager, Phi Chi. When interpreted through the codes 'Phi Chi' means: the Balanced Energy. The unconscious mind had the last say as to this wonderful woman's wisdom unfolding throughout the history of China. She reigned in all her wisdom, and what a gift she left us –

the legacy of the symbolism of the relationship of self! She had her workers build a beautifully decorated marble boat on the edge of the lake surrounding the Summer Palace; this boat serves to remind us all of the ship we will create within our self, which we will futuristically inherit as we glide our way through the consciousness of time, in order to create our own spaceship. Once we move up the ladder of our own DNA, where there is no room for us to create blunders.

The Summer Palace has 3,330 rooms and the Corridor of Records – which has the same explanation as the Akashic Records that have been passed on to us from Egypt – are coded with the 10,000 personalities of self, which are explained in the little stories painted on the ceilings and eaves as you walk throughout the length of this corridor. All of this explains, in story form, the Divine Inheritance of the emotions of life, as depicted through the DNA.

China has gifted back to the world a picture book explaining the stories in the Book of Revelations as foretold in the Holy Bible.

I have written the following passage earlier in my book "Decoding the Mind of God", before it was broken down into these nine separate books, therefore, I would like to repeat it here and add a section to it. The Tower of the Buddha's Fragrance is also coded with the Divine Inheritance. It represents our desire to become fulfilled through the emotional mind of the vagina. Remember that this just above the lungs of consciousness in the upper inner thighs explaining to us that this is the doorway of enlightenment. This temple houses the statue of the Bodhisattva, Guan Ean – which we now interpret in the English language as Quanyin (or "Khu-AN-Yin"); – do you see the similarity to the sounds of the Mayan language? She begins the journey as the Goddess of the Underworld, and she urges us up through the strength of her own action. This is why she is represented with many arms, which represent her wings in flight. These are the gifts she has earned for herself through her own inner yearning. Her partner's name is Guan Dong (or "Khu-AN-Dong"); he represents the penis, and he is known as the Lord of the Underworld.

Phi Chi's parting gift was to remove the previous emperor, who died at the age of thirty-eight. On the throne in his place, she put the next powerful thought, a three-year-old boy named Pu Yi. Wow! That is similar to the story of the "boy-king" of Egypt and also of the Dalai Lama, throughout the intellectual evolution of Tibet. Pu Yi stayed in power for the next thirteen years – until the Forbidden City was claimed through the rebellion of the ordinary people, who did not have the ability to understand how to open up their intelligence to evolve into their next level of ascension – or had never been shown how to do so. He never returned to the kingdom of his birthright.

All these stories are similar to the evolution of Ma'at in the Temple of Hathor in Egypt, as well as to the short introduction to Mary Magdalene in the Bible; that is, they all relate to the same sexual emotion. Those beings encoded their stories before we lived in order to leave behind the codes that would keep the evolution of our minds alive – in order for all of us to learn what humanity "must" learn.

Through their ego having to reign supreme, as a result of its own abasement for something that it could not find or understand within itself, we lost the original meaning of that hierarchical Collective Mind; thus, our life had to begin all over again. The ordinary people in China were overcome by their jealousy, and so they refracted from their responsibility through their ignorance of self. By denouncing the temple, they shattered their inner crystal of light and attacked their God within.

Your Notes:

CHAPTER FIFTEEN

The Mayan Principles

I realize that this tutorial becomes more involved as you read on – through my releasing so much information to you – but I also know that you have the rest of your life to understand these words that I have written! Why? For just as they were scribed within me, so, too, they are identically scribed within you. There is only one story!

Before I move on, I would like to bring in a few of the Mayan principles in order for you to see how this same story is repeated right through time and around the planet. The Mayan idea of the Universe is identical to the other Shamanic cultures, all of which explain to us the four directions of north, south, east, and west. The Mayans also had a concept of the underworld.

Their Lord of the Underworld was Xibalba. Let us look at the codes to interpret the name: "Chi-Bja-EL-Bja". This is the place of innocence, where we live until we begin to question our self. It is where we begin to unravel the codes to start our journey of self-discovery.

Another important name to explain is Kukulcan. Again, let us look at the codes to interpret: "Ku-Ku-EL-Kah-AN", or the "feathered serpent". In this coded word; we have two "Ku" syllables, which represent both hemispheres of the brain, and which stand for the words knowledge and understanding. We already recognize "EL" as "everlasting life"; "Kah" is "our inner knowledge becoming our life force"; and this ascends up through the middle kingdom of "AN", we know as "our education system".

The Mayan city of Teotihuacan is an interesting one to explain, as it brings many other cultures and languages together (i.e., China, ancient Rome, Japan, etc.). Once again, interpreted through the codes: "Teo (Tao-; Deo-; Dow)-Ti-Hu-Ark-AN". All of this shows us how this word represents "the education system of self, which is the storehouse of our intellectual light, also houses our Soul". Remember that we have named this area of our body as the solar plexus.

Explaining the Mayan names and codes further, we come to Topilitzin CeAcatl Quetzalcoatl, who was the son of the great Chichimeca ("Chi-Chi-Mecca") warrior named Mixcoatl. Through my interpretation, this story is similar to the story of the step-by-step guide of how Eli's name changed as he educated himself, becoming Elijah, Elias, and, finally, Elisha.

Chaak represents the old man who knew how to train his people; we know this because his representation sometimes showed him having four heads ("Cha-Ark"). Is this where the word Shaman originated from?

Let us consider the name of Quetzalcoatl again, this time by itself: "Que-Tza-EL-Ku-Art-EL", which interprets as, "where one begins to question one's self".

I could go on explaining all these codes to you for years! What is most important for you to understand is that the same story evolves in every land where the Collective Consciousness mathematically gathered this energy, as it had to be symbolically foretold in order for the future generations to be able to inherit themselves. Once you have understood how important it is to break up each word into syllables, you will have the time of your life reinvesting in the language of the Divinity of Babylon.

These same stories are still being repeated every day throughout all lands. When will we learn?! If we could understand this huge gift that we have been given, what could we realize for this wonderful place that we call home? We must bring out this hidden knowledge in order to be able to live our lives free of the temptations that are placed in front of us; for, this always confronts us, through others not understanding themselves. The lost temples of civilization are not lost – no one moved away or was destroyed; they never lived there in the first place! Those temples were built as "Mathematical Libraries" to echo our Higher Mind. We gaze at these temples and find a sense of peace in our mind as we are aware that they are explaining the heavenly abode.

The purpose of these temples was to provide a place for us to use in order to ascend our intelligence through the codes of understanding the evolution of hu-man, (man interprets as gene and men interprets as genes) as well as all the rest of the possibilities that await us. If we wish to describe all this with just one word, love is the only one we can use!

As you learn and earn your intelligence, you ascend up into your hierarchical mind, which creates a space in time that becomes yours, and the echo of your thoughts release out into the Collective Consciousness in order for the next person to hear your thoughts; thus, he/she may begin to understand his/her own Laws of Self – the Laws of his/her own Inner Universe – as they begin to unite their united verse.

Thank you for reading my written words, my precious reader. I have now introduced you to the worlds, or the written words, of "Extra-Terrestrial Intelligence". Your conscious understanding of all this will come in your own time; remember, the codes are already embedded in your unconscious.

Have a short pause now before you go on. A glass of water would also be beneficial!

Your Notes:

CHAPTER SIXTEEN

Contact With Extra-Terrestrial Intelligence

As we pause from viewing the Global Inheritance, hold my hand and come with me. Let's allow the story that we began with to catch up with this new, informative you. It is good for us to digress; we become much more aware of the past, and that is how we notice how this wonderful planet releases the same story from every thought we think!

Some of you easily see the image of an Extra-Terrestrial, while others cannot. Some see a flash of light but cannot decipher the ship. Others can only see the ship, while still others see an ET at the controls. As our intelligence collects through the freedom we have released from within, we are automatically swept up into the next stage of evolution; what you perceive all depends on the levels of your own intellect. You will see nothing if you have your own excusable parasites that desire to live off your Divine self. (Please refer to my book "Decoding Disease".)

The Collective Consciousness inherits and creates the life force of every species. It is explaining an inner language; every species is autonomically connected through their inherited mind – or DNA – in order to review the life force of the previous generations. In humans, the information is embedded in our glandular (endocrine) systems; it filters through to the pineal gland, where it becomes the crown we wear. When our mind opens, it becomes our own umbrella, which creates for us a form of hallowed ground that is always available. This Higher Self, which is part of the Collective, has always been within you. Through your own confidence collecting itself, you will realize its potentialities; you will learn how to rely on its judgment in order to become your intuition – or inner teacher – and this will remain within you until you die, or throughout my rendition, until you are ready to journey on to your next educated step.

This knowing creates and collects its own mathematical vibration; if every human is a spine of that huge umbrella of the Divine Consciousness, we can see that we are permanently connected to this dictionary of language. As it is below, so it is above. This huge dictionary has every thought embedded within it. Thus, as each human evolves into their own emotional heritage, through concentrating on their own self-worth, the transformation of each related word mirrors and reflects through that person's intellectual light, and this then returns into their futuristic thoughts. In other words, every spine of the Collective umbrella measures back through to the Oracle of that person who is thinking.

Remember that each thought we think is mathematically measured and released into the Collective as a form of cognitive energy. All this collects through the neural pathways, which dictate to the nervous system, and, from there, this becomes our library of consciousness. Here on earth, through understanding the mythical stories, we know this place as Alexandria – or, through the correct pronunciation, "EL-Ex-AN-Dri-EA" – which, when decoded through the Sacred Alphabet and Numerology, interprets as, "the Mind of God".

It is over forty-seven years since my first contact with the Extra-Terrestrial Intelligence (ETI). Since that first encounter, I have come to realize that as the intelligence encoded in my DNA unfolded, my body automatically learned to conclave through my endocrine system, extending up to and through the thymus gland and into the thyroid. From there, the four parathyroid glands harmonize all, creating a parabolic effect throughout my glandular system, consequently allowing me to stay balanced! I refer to these glands as my "Masters of Time". All of this occurs through the arcing of the geometrical mathematics, which I have created through arching up (ascending) into my covenant. This, in turn, has culminated from learning to speak and release my truth! If it matches to the truth of consciousness, I am given the green light to go on.

We all abide by this act as we reach up for the next breath; we cannot help but do this, as this is the place where we birth our truth – and that explains the arcing of our covenant, which God designed so that we must enter up into the unconscious mind through the medulla oblongata of our brain. The higher we exalt our mind, the more we realize how powerfully the truth of the Collective Consciousness is released throughout every cell.

***

There have been numerous stories written about personal experiences with the ET connection, including those regarding people who induced experiences by using drugs. What utter nonsense this is to the hierarchical mind! These individuals chose that attachment (the drug use) in their moment, and their own Higher Self gave back to them, through their own attendance, the message that they had to learn regarding their excuses. Drugs do not release our truth! Rather, drugs degrade the derivative that is released and reflected back to the individual from the Collective Consciousness. And, of course, all this happens in order to bring these people back to the awareness of their mind, which they have chosen to collapse into.

(A more detailed explanation of this journey will be revealed as you read on.) Drugs destroy the light in the cells, and this puts us on the path of the wanderer; the wandering of the ego can never return back to the original source of the Consciousness, or even to its own collective point. We have the ability to accomplish whatever we will for ourselves. Why? How? Simply through understanding that whatever has evolved and already exists on the earth, has evolved through humanity, and so we each have exactly the same measurement in our brain – we are all made up of the same identical energy. In other words, we are mirrors of one another. Hence, the use of psychotropic drugs that open the mind up to the point where the subject receives their intellectual equivalence – that is, they realize how they use, or abuse, their own intelligence.

Our glands are our caretakers; they hold our memories, and they will not allow this interference to seat itself up into the responsibility of the Divine Hierarchical Mind. Until we can understand the Law of Attraction at work throughout the Universe, we will hinder other people's interpretations of it, through accepting their own explanations of what they think the Law of God is. Once we step up into the realms of the "Royal Accolade" there can never be an excuse! Once we find our truth, we must hold to it; or until we find it, we must continue to seek it.

I could relate thousands of stories told to me by those who thought they saw "strange and frightening events". When I answered their questions, explaining the consequences of their stories to them, I could bring them back into their own truth. Once we did this together, they could relate to the justice of their thinking, and then they were very quickly able to forget their original story. Through their own masks, the Collective Consciousness gave back to them what they themselves had created, through their knowledge of what they thought was their intellectuality. People see different shapes, sizes, and faces of entities – each picture is given to them through the totality of their emotional intellect – how they view those entities depends on the amount of fear that is still trapped within them.

In other words, they will receive the visions that are suitable to be expounded upon and measured through their intellect, in order for them to best understand and learn. If you are promoting an excuse for yourself, the Universe will certainly oblige you. Over the years, I have looked at a very large vision of how our thoughts come alive to create the worlds that we escape into when we are in doubt. This occurs to assist those who reach out through the stuttering of their own mind.

***

Back to my own initial contact with Extra-Terrestrial Intelligence. I discovered the ETI in 1977 – on 11 November, to be exact – when they arrived on my property in Australia that evening. I was milking the cows at the usual time, and I had just nestled into the flanks of my favourite cow, Sarah. She liked to be the first one in line and the first into the bales, and she did not like hanging around waiting. We had a special affinity, and, as I communicated with her, she would moan softly to me when she agreed – or snort if she disagreed – with my thinking. We complemented one another, and I would always ask her permission to drop her milk until my hands got into action. My usual conversation began with, "Right Oh, my girl – let's rock on and get it over with." I would start humming a tune to her as she came closer and grew comfortable, and then she would lean against the shed wall as I nestled into her flank, and our odours blended as her sweet milk flowed into the bucket.

That particular evening, my thoughts were jumbled; I needed this time to be alone to work out where I was up to. The milking of my cows was my meditation at the end of the working day, before I went up to the house and to tackle the evening meal, baths, homework, etc. I focused on my hand movements, as I loved to watch the mathematics one used for releasing the milk. I placed one hand around each teat, holding my hand up high under the udder, and then, starting with my little finger and working each stroke up to the index finger, I squeezed, and the milk would flow. I followed my daily mathematics that evening; soon, my rhythm began to pick up, and the milk was flowing in a steady stream into the bucket. Just then I felt these subtle vibrations up and down my spine.

At first, I thought that Jack the Snake, must have been close by, but, when I looked around, he wasn't there. Jack was a harmless 3.3-metre-long python that lived in the dairy, and his job was to keep the rats out of the grain bins. When he moved along the rafters and came up close to where I was milking, he would swing down and sway behind me. I could always sense when Jack was behind me. It is amazing how, when our mind is focused and still, our sixth sense just takes over. When that happens, we feel another energy enter our own, and we call this sensation ESP. Feeling this – and how strongly you feel it, if at all – depends on the focus of your mind; that is, whether your mind is working for you. In any case, when I "sensed" Jack, I would squirt some milk up at him, and he would sway down, open his mouth, and have a drink. Jack had a unique energy, it was long and kind of like a groan; it took time for his vibrations to move throughout the length of his whole body. That night, the vibrations that I was feeling continued up and down my spine, and I relaxed into them. To be honest, at that time, I imagined that it was something between me and Sarah – just the cow and I nurturing one another and becoming one – once I determined that Jack was nowhere inside. The next thing I remember was coming to – it seemed like moments later, but I felt like I had been out or away. I looked into a full bucket with five gallons of fluffy milk filled right to the top. I still had the same cow in the bale. I became embarrassed, as I must have really stripped her udder until it was empty, and there was nothing left for her little calf. I moved the bucket out over against the shed wall and let her out of the bale, explaining to her that I was sorry and must have fallen asleep for a few minutes. I felt contentment surge through my body, followed by a sense of peace that I wanted to last forever.

I put the other calves onto their mothers, as I certainly had enough milk to feed the family until the following morning's milking. Sarah's little calf nestled in and head-butted her mother. As I saw the look of contentment on the calf's face, I knew that Sarah had found a reserve supply to satisfy her next in line. I opened the gate to let the cows out of the yards, and I noticed three lights bobbing around in the paddock on the other side of our creek. This large creek was the children's swimming hole, as well as our irrigation supply, and it was some 40 metres wide. It meandered through the paddocks, around a bend, and into the waterfalls, after which, it stretched out over the land. These lights that I saw appeared about twenty metres on the flat land on the other side of the creek.

My first thought was to wonder why my boys were out there and what they were doing with the pressure lamps. I called out to them, but they did not respond. However, my calling attracted my husband's attention. He was working on a tractor in the large machinery shed nearby, and he came over to me. We were in the middle of another drought at that time, and I said to my husband, "Look at those boys with the pressure lamps! I hope they are careful, as the grass is tinder dry, and we don't need a fire at this time of year." He explained that the boys were up at the house, not over in the paddock, and then he, too, became inquisitive about the lights. He picked up the bucket, told me what a good girl I was, and took it up to the house. I tidied up the milking shed and put fresh lucerne in the bales for the morning's milking session.

My family had come up from the south to spend Christmas with us, and the house was busy and full of laughter. My husband thought that maybe someone was trying to maverick one of our cows for their own Christmas, so he went back inside to talk and gather the men. They constructed a plan as to which way they could surround those people who were so blatantly close to the house with their lights. The women meandered down to the cattle yards and sat up high on the slip rails of the fence, watching as the men came around to block all the entrances.

Off the men went towards the paddock, approaching from different directions in trucks and tractors and on motorbikes. As they approached the area, the ring of lights lifted up off the ground and hovered above the trees. The men stopped dead in their tracks to view the phenomenon. The lights started dancing around in the sky, but, as my husband walked towards them, they took off over the hill.

The men came back to the house in awe of what they had just seen, and we all sat down to one of the quietest evenings that we had shared in a long time.

At that time, I had cervical cancer, which my doctor was treating. However, a few days after that first ET contact, I came to the realization that my cancer had disappeared. I did not know what had happened or why, but I could feel a gentle lightness within me; I felt different and at peace with myself. Allowing that feeling to just sit with me for a bit, after Christmas when the house was back in order, I made an appointment and went back to my doctor. He did some tests, and then he informed me that I was in remission. My mathematics had equalized, and so the old energy no longer had a place to feed from. That healing that I had received, produced a huge window in my mind, where I received a second opportunity to reshape my thoughts and begin my life again.

I'd always had a thirst for knowledge; this time, I wanted to gulp it down as quickly as I could digest it. I went to every course available for women in the Outback, learning floristry, cake decorating, calligraphy, pottery, and home decorating. I collected a vast array of "first prize" certificates at the yearly show, and I felt pleased and happy. These achievements gave me a variety of tools that I felt content to have, and that I could use to support me in my efforts to improve my home and family, which was important to me at that stage of my life. My inner nurturing became complete.

The lights made contact again two years later (in 1979) at my daughter's engagement party. As the guests danced into the night, those three bright blues (different colour this time) lights appeared, dancing in the sky over our farm house to the beat of our music, and the time, 11.11 pm. We had invited 120 people that evening, and this phenomenon stunned them all. The locals laughed and cheered at the movement of those lightships swaying in the night sky.

My husband and a friend hopped into a car and drove towards them, and, whoosh! The lights disappeared very quickly over the hill and out of sight. This unexpected event left the families who had travelled from interstate dumfounded and panic began to take hold. The local residents took over, reassuring them that they were accustomed to these phenomena, as it had been part of their lives as long as they could remember. No harm was done. Later, we discovered that our location was situated on a power ley line or grid, where a power station would be built in the years to come. As you can imagine, it took some time for everyone to regain their composure and return to dancing. That second contact took away any remaining fear that I harboured as to Extra-Terrestrial Intelligence. Through my belief and personal growth I had given to myself, I had completed the next stage of the program designed on my behalf in order to my benefit and satisfaction.

The lessons I earned this time were in regard to my having to disconnect from my daughter, as she had chosen to create a new life and was about to be introduced into another tribe. She was now becoming my emotional age, and her thoughts were focusing on her new life and future. I say that my daughter was my "emotional age", as she had now become a woman who was learning to experience her own freedom in order to begin her next inherited mind.

I went on to rear my other children to adulthood, and then I became emotionally driven to begin this quest. My life changed rapidly; I had to reawaken the daughter in me, and that gave me the possibility to step forward into my next world. I am sure that I returned back to the budding teenager, as everything seemed to be a challenge for me – that is, my life had expanded to include every possibility that released from the recesses of my mind.

I, the student, was ready; thus, the teachers began to appear, placed before me to explain the things that I did not understand. Much of my journey I have already recollected for you, although in the pages that follow, I will explain more to you in regard to the lessons I derived from these teachers.

Your Notes:

CHAPTER SEVENTEEN

The Teachers

My friend and teacher, Swami Dharmavidyananda, came into my life; she explained the philosophy of the Eastern traditions and the principles of Buddhism. She began to show me how I could satisfy my emotional self through understanding and balancing the inner mind; how I could achieve a quieter mind, and how this connection to my inner heaven could enrich my thinking.

Her teachings moved on through the arts of yoga and meditation. I began to understand my own muscular system, and I learned how to stretch and ease my inner tension. This was when I began to realize the importance of learning how to balance myself. This was my introduction to my Higher Self; it was my own energy that I had not formally been aware of up to that point. In short, I learned to love and respect me. I was being introduced to God on a personal level; I tried to feel at ease with this information, as the more I listened, I also knew that it was very important.

In the beginning of my journey, I began to speak of my new knowledge to my father, hoping that he would not think I was crazy. Taking away all my fear, he began with; "Did you know that humanity, as a whole, has still not answered the first question ever asked? Intrigued, I inquired, "What was that question?" He replied, "Why am I here? Think about it and I will ask you again in half an hour's time." He went on to explain that these reflections of thought had been his own beliefs when he was around fourteen years of age. He left home from Chrystal Brook, in South Australia at twelve years of age and rode his push-bike to Cairns in the most northern part in Queensland over 1,800 miles. Along the way, he earned his keep by undertaking a medley of tasks for food and shelter and money, over a four year period. He then spent six months learning from a healer who travelled from Sweden to open up his healing centre in the rain forest just out of Cairns. My father informed us children that he became a "Jack of all Trades" during his long ride. He also spoke fondly of the friends he made through his teenage years. This remarkable chapter in his life unfolded before the onset of the Second World War. He proceeded to recount a profound lesson: "When the student is prepared, the teacher invariably appears." Undoubtedly, his path took a distinct turn at sixteen when he altered his age and enlisted to serve in the war.

My father became my teacher, explaining to me how to understand the flow of energy in the body, as he had received this same teaching and training all of those years before! He explained how our mind works when it is naked of thought – that is, when no false garment covers and protects it, as such garments are the things we so quickly use as disguises to mask our inner truth.

He taught me methods of healing others, especially how we could release their blocked energy by moving our hands through their aura. His instruction covered how to read the electrical circuit of energy that each human has; by tracing their flow of energy, through our senses aligning with their blocked thoughts, working to correct and reshape the client's thinking. Explaining to the client how to focus inward, blockages could be dissolved. Through the client's understanding, he/she allows the unconscious/higher mind to overflow, this in turn releases endorphins, which return back to them, as they accept their own gratitude for that which they have sometimes refused, forgotten, or didn't know how to give to themselves.

The mathematics of the mind always add up on your behalf, reaching a "peak of the moment performance", and this is where your own illusion mirrors back to you an equality of same grace. At that point, if you have the urge and interest to go on, you are automatically introduced up into the next level of your eclectic learning. You have the canvas to manifest for yourself the how, why, and what of your aspirations in life.

My father explained that inside our body, we each have electromagnetic ley lines that resonate with the Earth's grid, interconnecting with the meridian lines, all of which explains how and why we walk and talk. He made it all sound very simple as he explained how the healing energies release from within; creating the potential for us to open new doorways to all the available worlds of intelligence. He then connected this to the biblical account of St. Luke, who, at the age of twelve, was referred to as the world's youngest doctor. I stood before him, all five feet of me, feeling like the tallest person in the world, and asked him why he had never shared this gift with me before. His reply was simple: "You have never asked me before!"

My cherished father passed away a few days later. He told me as he was leaving my home that when he died, he would hand his reigns over to me to carry on in his name, as I was his and my mother's "star seed". My gentle mother followed him ninety days later. It was during this time I received an unexpected visitor named Ross, on my doorstep. He held a large crystal gemstone from Shirley MacLaine in Peru. He explained that she had a message for me, indicating that my next guide was waiting to introduce himself. As you've previously read, my first encounter was with an extraterrestrial and ten little ones during an evening of meditation. They shared insights about the Attaché' case we carry to support us.

***

At the beginning of our quest, we are introduced to another section of the world that is opposite from our own. It is through this attainment that we humans can reach our future without the dilemmas that we create along the way. Many people, when coming into the connection of self with an enquiring mind, have an urge to take a journey to Egypt, Tibet, China, Japan, India or Peru. We have an urge to reach out away from our homeland. Why? We need to search for our opposite; maybe we have a desire to taste the unknown and stretch our boundaries to see how far we can go. And then we must begin to connect with the four corners – from the south to the north, and from the west to the east – that is the square becoming the circle, in which we search for information regarding the Medicine Wheel, which represents the Laws of the Collective.

In the beginning of my journey, I tried four times to go to India and Tibet with friends who wanted to return to the wisdom of the other side of the world; it never eventuated for me. Either my car would not start, as the battery became mysteriously flat, and so I missed my plane; or I got to the airport, but there wasn't a seat available for me. The same experience kept on repeating itself. I became angry and screamed at God, "Why can't I go? I want to attend!" I wanted to keep up with the masses, and I wanted to share my new experiences with others of same mind.

The Universe delivered a message for me in all this, of course, as to why I could not attend those countries. I began to realize that I had to find the answers within me, and so I humbly apologized for my behaviour and began again. I listened to my friends' descriptions when they returned, and I found that I could learn and understand their stories by finding my own answers within myself. Now I am free to travel the planet, and, in each country that I journey into, as an invited guest, I realize that I am as they are. I am treated like "royalty" when I enter other lands, and I reciprocate accordingly.

From there, I went into the journey head-on, full of praise for myself and wonderment at what my possibilities were; my yearning for self had moved me forward. The healing worlds opened up, and into them I swam, learning many different modalities and realizing that each one advanced a step past the other!

I was brought back to earth very quickly when my next teacher, Renate, entered my life. She foretold the arrival of five white dolphins who would impart to me a wisdom that was pure and extremely rare. As a result, I looked for these dolphins for a long time – through books, magazines, cards, calendars, and various sources. I could find pictures with three dolphins, but never with five. I searched this way for more than two years, but nothing came to me. Finally, as my intelligence began to release and unfold, I encountered those five white dolphins on the beach, an experience I detail in my book "Decoding the Dolphin's Breath".

Next came Sharon, who transported me back two thousand years, initiating my introduction into the metaphysical language. My goodness, I did not understand a word! Throughout my days with Sharon, I became panic-stricken and horrified many times. When things didn't work the way, I wanted them to; I would run to Sharon with questions. Her answer would be, "Don't ask me why this didn't work for you. You did not understand and collect your thinking correctly before you asked! Be silent. Allow God his turn, and then all will be revealed to you at exactly the right time." Oh boy, again! I heard those words many times from Sharon during the years that followed.

Over the next few years, as I took my journey into the dark night of my Soul, my fear screamed for attention many times, and I would run to Sharon with an excuse in order to find the courage to go on. "Yes, I can give you five minutes of my time," she would say to me. I would almost yell at her when I said, "I need help! I have so many questions." She would say, "Well, I will have the most important one now, and, if you give me the right question, you will find that the rest will answer you on behalf of themselves." Oh boy! Sharon never made any excuses; she was a very thorough and wonderful teacher.

Vicki came into my life from another land in order to teach me the story of Esoteric Intelligence. I had difficulty at first in accepting this truth, as it seemed to come from another world, far beyond my own beliefs. I had to take a huge step forward and leap into the depths of my own faith to understand what Vicki had to teach me. That forward thinking led me into the realms of Astrology, Tarot, Palmistry, and Dream Interpretation. All this was what I had considered "the unknown" prior to that time; I had not explored any these fields before, and yet I had to accept that I already "knew" all of it on a higher level – that is, in my Higher Mind. I had to step up, not down or out, in order to step into understanding that my intellect had many layers.

Next Helena from a country in Europe arrived and came into my life. She explained the confusion (perplexity) of humanity, and how we create this confusion through our ignorance and misinterpretation of the Laws of God. What are we doing? Where are we promoting a positive future? How can we understand our self? How can we help humanity understand the self? All this ignorance, misinterpretation, and lack of understanding depreciates the entire Collective. Helena illuminated the concepts of darkness and the light to me. She explained how I could discern through my thinking before I committed myself to speak, and how I could do likewise before I chose the direction to take. From her, I learned that I perpetually held the opportunity to guide myself onward. She was always available to me – always there for me when I needed her the most.

Helena taught me about "Trekking", which meant stepping my energy outside myself; in other words, I had to learn to see with closed eyes. She introduced me to Telepathic Communication, which connects to the wonderful world of Shamanism, sweeping us into it. Helena also informed me that I would receive extreme Spiritual messages over the years that will follow, and that these were mine and mine alone. She said, "People will not understand you at first; they will turn their back on you. Only when your journey has finished can you permit yourself to talk your walk. You will be guided for the rest of your life; doorways will be filled with availabilities, and opportunities will open up for you. As you think, there it will be! Be like Peter the apostle, 'Build and create it, and they will come.' People will come to you by the thousands to hear you explain how you earned your inner knowledge."

***

It was hard for me to digest and accept that we are protected by the Laws of the Universe (Collective Consciousness) for the rest of our lives, when we make a commitment to accept this inner journey. I thought I had done a darn good job for the first forty odd years, and I looked forward to taking it easy for the next forty. Oh boy! How wrong I was!

The Collective Consciousness could also be referred to as the Collective Inner Science. In other words, this inner science explains how the outer science shaped itself; we understand our self through understanding those who have walked before us, and by understanding them, we come to understand our

Self – and the Universe – even more. I had difficulties in understanding and accepting that the word science ("sci-essence") is created through the acceptance of balancing the energy of the Collective, as the Collective creates the essence of the microscopic worlds, which, in turn, create the macrocosmic evolution.

With my heart now wide open, I thank every one of my teachers, who have all returned home for their next educated learning. Their invaluable gifts of knowledge and wisdom have enlightened me, providing many stories to share with my students when they enter my "Sciential (to know the knowing) Centre" which relaxes them when they hear of my own shortcomings, when I began!

I remind my students that this passage represents – "the journey of the road less travelled" - there are mountains to overcome – roads with boulders that have to be removed - rivers to cross, some fast flowing, others with a trickle - and all must be attended too. As they embark on a brand new journey, with a smile on their face, they will carve new highways for their evolution into the wonderment of the Laws of the Universe, which have been here since our time first began.

Your Notes:

CHAPTER EIGHTEEN

The "Echo-Inside-Essence"

The Extra-Terrestrial Intelligence returned again in 1991, twelve years after its last appearance in my life (during my daughter's engagement party). This event in 1991 occurred one night after 120 days of my being in a trance-like state; during that time, I had talked to hundreds of people who knocked on my door, twenty-four hours a day. Throughout these previous days, I had to learn to become an open trance channel, where I seemed to have become robotic in all of my endeavours. I was permanently plugged into the Collective Consciousness; I could hear and relate to all of it, but I still tried to go about my own business at the same time.

People walked through my house, day and night; I did not even know most of them. They wanted to listen, share, ask questions, or be healed; they were searching for answers to their own pent-up emotions. To begin with, it was just the local people, and then it expanded to people from different areas of the state and all over the country; after a while, they started to come from other countries, near and far. They all just wanted to share their stories with someone who understood.

I never sent out an invitation, so how did they know where I lived? Their unconscious mind, unknown to their conscious selves, had directed them to my house. Some call this coincidence; my term for it is how we "echo-inside-essence", which relates to God's nurturing – you are always in the right place, at the right time; there is never a mistake.

The Laws of Attraction introduced themselves to me so that I could learn to release these wonderful twelve Disciplines – or Disciples – the twelve strands of my DNA inside me. My body began to communicate back to me; I had begun to release the "language of the body", which is the storehouse where we have inherited and collected the language of the unconscious mind. This telepathic agreement is in every human, and it is our cosmic cord – or pathway – to God. All these events kept the locals occupied; I figured that, if they were talking about me, they were leaving someone else alone. I had found an inner sense of security that shielded me from other people's cruel words, so that they no longer affected me the way that they once had. My inner strength was collecting, building my character and creating intelligence within me; all this was coming to order so that I could become stronger and more collective. In short, I was learning to create my own strength of body, mind, and Soul.

I was learning to heal the human body through the energy fields that vibrated within each person. My father's gentle teachings were beginning to make sense, and as I understood more and more, I helped more and more. I found that I could easily read people's disturbed energy, and I knew which part of the body released their fear; I could see and watch the colours manifest in their aura, which helped me notice the changes that they created through their thinking.

Every moment of my life released a new wisdom to add to the words of my inner dictionary. The worlds of healing create an extreme religious experience in the self. I found that I was being brought up into the higher Shamanic resonances of what we refer to as "psychic surgery". This level awakens in us when we have connected in totality with the unconscious mind; the Elders of my twelve tribes began to release and come alive. My Apostles were beginning to work on my behalf.

I did not have to think too much; I was moving through my own state of grace, and people always waited on my doorstep to be healed, twenty-four hours a day. Some of them could not even speak English, but this was never a problem, as words were not needed between us. I could see through their layers of confinement, as my inner eye had gradually opened up to view the world in 3D; I knew exactly where their blocked energy had collected, and for what reason. Once I made myself known to the fears that their ego had wrapped around itself, the healing could commence.

It was a magnificent era of my life; once you have lived this experience, there is no possible way that you could ever walk away from the glory of self! They were brought into my healing room, placed on the table, and, three minutes later, they walked out – completely healed. It was during this time that I entered into the worlds of "coma", (i.e., as to how we collect our mathematics, in order to be placed in our own sanctuary so that we can rest from the inner turmoil). This is an autonomic reaction delivered to us, once again, from the unconscious mind. I had an idea of what went on, as, a few months before I began the journey; I had entered into my own diabetic coma. It only lasted for a few days, but I could vividly remember my thinking as I came out of it to face the world again. I remembered having been in the land of China, where I had learned so many different stories, and where I had met these wonderful High Priests clothed in the most magnificent robes. They were from the Divine equation of the Collective. I felt like St John the Divine, in the Book of Revelations, when God tells him to open up the inner seven churches of Asia. I felt someone slapping my face as I came out of the coma, and I opened my eyes to see a beautiful Chinese woman standing over me and calling my name.

My first words to her were, "Thank you for being here and for the gifts that you have bestowed upon me." She was shocked at first, but then, once I answered the preliminary questions satisfactorily– that is, knowing my name, where I was, my date of birth, and where I lived – she asked me to tell her what I could remember about where I had just been. For the next couple of hours I spoke of my experiences, explaining my stories to her. She wrote it all down, asking if she could use the information in her current education – of course I said yes!

Some months later, when I was using the Shamanic inferences, all that information filtered back and released into my mind. I had to totally accept and have faith in the way that my mathematics were changing and advancing the images I was receiving. This was all I had to rely on.

I began to understand why we choose to go into a coma when we reach the end of the excuses we are so busily creating. It all has to do with the ego losing its control over us, as we need sleep in order to release the pressure of the ego – or the left brain. When the ego cannot rule, we need to sleep – or be put to sleep, through our mathematical equations, in order for the turmoil to cease and our mind to rest. Have you ever noticed that, when you have had an exciting day, you need to be able to rest the mind before you go to sleep? Things need to be switched off before the mind eases itself into a restful mode. So, when the ego has reached its own zenith, we urge ourselves into a natural repose, where our feelings release a sense of tranquillity, which, in time, learns to reign supreme.

This new education that I had received from my teachers was now becoming a part of my existence, and my life had totally changed forever. I could feel these eclectic experiences working with me, and I knew that I would never return to the old me – in other words, my excuses were a thing of the past. My inner clarity reigned supreme. I liked this new me; my friends looked at me through different eyes, and they trusted me.

Back to the start of this story. On that night, after 120 days in my trance- like state, my students walked in with smiles on their faces, asking what I had been up to. They said that they could see my home very clearly from a distance, as it had a large ball of light around it that seemed to glow in the dark. I had up to twenty students who came to my home every week for meditation and communication. We settled down, I gave my meditation, they asked their questions, and I answered them. The topic for that evening was "Relationship"; on that particular night, time just slipped away.

Suddenly, we heard two knocks on the front door, so one of my students got up and opened it; nobody was there. As soon as he had closed the door and sat down again, we heard two knocks on the back door; again, nobody was there. The students thought that somebody was playing games with us. After a long moment, we heard two more knocks on the front door, and another student quickly opened it. To our surprise, a mist came rolling through the open door, and we saw eleven Aliens coming through the mist and into my lounge room.

Of the eleven, ten were short, and one was tall. The time was 11:11 p.m., and it was 11 November 1991 (11-11-1991). Remember that my first ETI experience happened on 11-11-

1977. (For a more detailed explanation on numbers, please read my book "Decoding The Sacred Alphabet and Numerology"). I had not prepared this image myself; through the layers of my own confinement, my eternal energy had collected with the plasmic consciousness. This is called the Essence of God! My energy had finally reached up and connected with the highest form of the Collective Consciousness.

Only three of us in that group could see the holographic image of the Aliens, as we had all become ensconced into the fourth dimension through understanding their vibrational thinking. Some of the other students could only see the mist, as their fear, which had not yet abated, had already taken control of their thinking. The newer students just rolled over and went to sleep. Their barriers had jumped to attention as soon as the mist entered the room, and the phenomenon had blocked their inner sight. Their Horus – or third eye – had become blinded, and their shutters were down. You only fear for yourself. Remember, please: If you think it, you create it, and then it will become!

The tallest Alien told me that his name was Pharaohtriea – or "Pha-Rha-O-Tri-EA" – and he came through into my world. (Please refer to the codes in my book "Decoding The Sacred Alphabet and Numerology", in order to understand his name.) He explained that he was a member of the "Brotherhood of Light" which I had never heard of; he told me that they were all from a planet of emerald-green situated in the eastern galaxies. Their emerald-green planet was next to the blue planet. Their home was a planet of hope, love, and service – who could fear that? I later understood that the colour of emerald-green represented my emotional self. On the Medicine Wheel and in the principles of Shamanism, the east symbolically represents the worlds within.

Pharaohtriea was tall, light, and so very gentle; he communicated to me with compassion and love. I felt that emotion course through every cell in my body. I call him a "male energy", as he spoke to me in a low, melodious, masculine voice. He said, "Have no fear; I mean no harm to you. I am as you are. You and I are of same mind in this moment, and, with your trust in me, we can become one." He smiled. As his small mouth moved, I felt the subtle energy flow throughout my body. I felt comfortable, as his vibration was so calm. "When you can find your faith in me, as I have in you, we will then have the opportunity to communicate as one," he said.

The group became quiet and subdued. They looked to one another in anticipation, and, through their support of each other, their fear began to relax. Although they still could not see, they could feel the energy in the room change to a gentle coolness. The entrance of these beings into my home had made a great difference to the inside temperature. It was a hot 35 degrees Celsius outside, but now the students were looking for blankets or beach towels, to wrap themselves in. They had placed their shock around them for protection, so their fear was in attendance. I realized that the Universal Consciousness was preparing me for another paradigm shift in my own consciousness; as always, I became a willing subject.

I had been waiting in anticipation for this since 1979 – finally! – my moment had come. I asked Pharaohtriea why he was there, and he explained that I was ready to evolve and receive my next shift of consciousness. I was more than ready. The last 120 days had been, literally, mind-blowing; I had moved into realms of thought that I could have never created through my own thinking. What more could I expect? I had let this loving feeling flow through me, and I never wanted it to cease!

CHAPTER NINETEEN

An Attaché Case

Earlier in the evening, my students and I had exchanged views on the topic of "Relationship". Their questions ranged the gamut, including: How great is my responsibility to others and myself? How far could this expand in me without interfering with who I am? Can I live my life and accomplish all without having to share it with someone else? What is "permanence", and how can we understand it emotionally? Do I have to stay faithful to one person all of my life, and, if so, why? When is the right time to commit to only one? Oh! I envy the thoughts of the young mind. When I was their age, if only those questions had entered my mind! If only I'd had then the same opportunity that they had now to seek the answers to those questions!

The group consisted people mostly in their twenties, some in their early thirties. They were university students – they studied business administration, nursing, medicine, forensic science; others among them were young priests and nuns, as well as some biblical scholars and students of other religions. In other words, they were educated young people who had a deeper interest in what had already been written; they were searching for – and hoping for – answers to their questions. They yearned for a more advanced interpretation of the Oracle of Life – that is, an understanding of why we are here on this planet.

Pharaohtriea asked for and received permission to speak to the group. He and I both adjusted our energies, and he then proceeded to speak to the group through me. I didn't panic; I just allowed him entry, finding him to be an easy and gentle energy to blend with. His voice was quiet; his breath was gentle, and it tasted of the crispness of the high mountains. I smelt the essence of the fir trees. It felt like I was communicating with someone in a dream.

After introducing himself to them, he explained that he was a consciousness for the next opportunity that was available to all of humanity, and, when they had enough faith in themselves, they could learn from him. He said that every human with a yearning to learn more about themselves, has the opportunity to evolve into this next step of understanding; furthermore, he explained that, when the time was right for each of them, it would automatically begin to shape into their own consciousness.

He chose to speak about "Attachment", which he explained as follows:

"An attaché case is something that you carry your personal documents in, and those documents represent your collective strength and character up to that moment; they are the importance of what you have worked and strived for. Your worlds of the past and present are correlating mathematically to create your future intelligence, and all your thoughts are placed in that case. The responsibility that is created from achieving this experience is your future releasing itself, which fortifies your gratuity. You never want to let it out of your sight, so you fix your attention to it. It is a relationship with the self.

Relationship with one another is the same, and, when you begin to walk towards a new relationship, feelings of contentment awaken in you; this takes over your thinking worlds, as it is something new, something that has stimulated your feelings and attracted your attention. It gives you a sense of freedom and light-heartedness. Your natural urge is to hold it close, to claim it as your own and never let it go. It can take over your thinking, where you seem to lose all sense of direction. You have a tendency to call that feeling "Love". This attachment is something that has to be understood, fostered, and then allowed to grow naturally. How can your attaché case fill with your worthy documents in just five minutes?

If you begin to feel responsible and committed to this new relationship, the energy of your thoughts begins to change. Through your innocence, your freedom becomes a form of yearning – a sexual urge – and those urges influence your character, causing you to want to take responsibility on behalf of your self. You want to share your communicative thoughts and add to one another. You must learn to watch that you don't over control, lest you lose the wisdom of this precious gift that you are striving to give to one another; and, in turn, you need to learn to receive, as well as give.

Let us now look at what we call "Sharing." Where does it fit with "Attachment"? To share something, or someone, alerts us to the fact that two energies of the same attention are equalizing with each other at the point where they are reimbursed back to self. This attraction is a reward of greater benefit to your life. Sharing is the improved quality of life. Attachment comes through understanding the sharing, and we add this to the relationship. Love is the preciousness of Sharing, Balancing and Harmonizing. Allow time to be your teacher."

He thanked me for my participation, and then he gently withdrew his energy.

The other ten beings walked around and the room filled with laughter at their antics; they subtly touched the students who could not see them, yet could sense – or feel – their energy. After a while, the mist gently left the room, and we watched as it disappeared through the keyhole of the front door. A subtle silence filled the room, and no one moved. We all had been completely unprepared for this event. The temperature began to rise again, and those students whom the energy shift had put to sleep began to stir.

My students floated out the door that night and were never the same again. They spoke about that experience for months, realizing that they had been shown the opportunity to create their own time. If love with self could return these benefits – and love with someone else could grow and mature this way – where was the penance of his/her future?

I have had the pleasure of seeing all those students again during the last thirty odd years, and they all are finding their own contentment now – and they all still talk to me about that night. They have gone onward and upward with their businesses, teachings, become university lectures, and whatever paths they have pursued. Some have written books about how those evenings helped them understand this inner gift that we each can give to our self.

In other words, they all have succeeded in their life through having allowed time to correctly fill their attaché cases.

Your Notes:

CHAPTER TWENTY

The Philosopher's Stone

When Pharaohtriea returned three days later, I was alone; that is when my new life with him began. I found that total seclusion was going to be the only way for me to adjust to this time warp without the interference of others. I felt safe and comfortable with my exalted friend who showed me an immense respect; and, the more interested and preoccupied I became with his teachings, the more contented I felt. I was neither hungry nor thirsty. The Oracle of my Truth had begun to release inside me – I did not need any other sustenance. My mind began to tune in to different frequencies, where time seemed irrelevant to my everyday existence. I had begun to return back to the original source.

Sleep became a thing of the past; through the knowledge that I was beginning to accept and understand, I found that my ego could no longer demand or detain me. My life never felt strained; everything happened at exactly the right moment, and I was always in the right place, at the right time. My bodily functions worked perfectly without me creating an excuse for what I did not know or understand. My hunger diminished; at that time, I did not realize that I wasn't eating – that is how committed my mind was to my lessons. I recall now the day when I began to notice that the same food had been in the fridge for days, and then a memory flooded into my mind that maybe I had not nourished myself. I tried to eat an apple or a few strawberries every three weeks or so, in the beginning, through my realizing that I still had an old fear remaining as to trusting this new life explicitly. Do you remember the old saying, "An apple a day keeps the Doctor away!"?

At this time, my teachings were taking me deeper into the language of the Collective, and I learned that each country had its own language for both its spoken and written word. First, I was to listen to how they pronounced their syllables and words; from there, I was taught to understand how these people dressed – the garments they wore; the symbolic structure embroidered around the neck and hem of their garments; the stories they told, and where and how they expressed the deep desire to pass on to each forthcoming generation. Why was each story important? If it was important to the parent, why did they feel that it must be important to their offspring? If the parent had already attained the story, it did not ever need to be mentioned again, as the child already had that knowledge instilled within him/her.

From there, we moved into their kitchens in order to understand what they placed on their table and what was available for them to eat. Through the pronunciation of their language to one another, I could realize what part of their Alchemy they used to support their spoken word, as well as how they repeated their day-to-day existence with one another. To equate the country as a whole, they needed certain foods to sustain them. Each language used the same vegetables and meat; although, to find their compatibility to communicate with one another, the preparation of their dishes differed. The herbs, spices, legumes, and grains were added; all of which had to become a resonance that was appropriate for the way they pronounced each word. When they realized that a member of their tribe was out of balance, the first thing they did was to change their food. Their religious endeavours played the greatest part to their tribal inheritance. It was the connection as to how they were attaining their conversation between each other on an inner level that supported their belief in themselves, not what was appearing on an outer frequency. Now we can begin to see how all these tools were being brought together to sustain each language. Remember that the mathematical essence of everything we place in our mouth is released as we chew our food. The essence that releases is absorbed up through the two little holes on the roof of our mouth; from there, it travels up and into the pituitary gland, where it is measured and scribed into the Alchemy of our brain.

I had a huge undertaking to understand the Alchemy of the brain. This was a new world and a tremendous task for me to accept. Thank God for those massage courses earlier on where I could understand the anatomy and the nervous system of the human body. I began to realize the importance of Helena's words, "Trust, and all will be revealed." These wonderful chemical elements that we are all born with begin to activate when we are asleep, through the ego – or left brain – being in abeyance to itself. I found that while I was awake, I could watch and listen to this matter conforming to its own principle. The Philosopher's Stone is right inside us all, and every one of us has the power to release and reclaim it. Remember the myths? We are all King Arthur claiming a relationship to our intellect, which is explained as the hidden city of Avalon.

For more than three years, I had no sleep. If it worried me, I took two to three minutes to close my eyes and slip into a meditation of silence. I found that, during those moments, I could watch my body repairing itself. It was fascinating to watch as the glands began to vibrate and urge the energy through my ley lines to the weaker sections of my body. When that energy became clear, a little blue light switched on inside, and all was well. I can laugh about all this now, but, at that time, I was extremely dedicated to my endeavours as a student; of course, I had to do it right.

Pharaohtriea's first request of me was this, "We ask you to read the Holy Book. There are stories explained in there that you now comply with; through the advanced awakening of your inner resonance you have the possibility to unravel and add more sophistication that is needed for the growth of this wonderful place you call home." This came as quite a shock to me, and, at first, I refused his request. I had grown up with the Bible on the table after each meal, and I was now searching for something different; I wanted the "New Age"!

My thought was that if I did what he asked of me, it was going to drag me back into my past. So, as the teenager within me rebelled, I cried, "I'm not ready for this – no way!" I'd had enough difficulty as a child trying to understand the language of that book, so why should I be bothered trying again now? Over the next few days, I thought, "Maybe things have changed, and I do not need to hang onto some of my old beliefs. Maybe I have to grow up! Why is the Bible so important in this world? Maybe it has something different to add." I also knew that I could not deny his request, so I gave in, and retrieved my old Bible from its hiding place.

As I began to accept my new awakening to this knowledge, I changed Pharaohtriea's name to "the Architect". That name re-entered my psyche from my childhood. This "Being of Light" reminded me of the story of Moses, and I had learned as a child that he was the Architect of Egypt. Moses designed buildings, strengthening and adding to the city to make it stronger, brighter, and larger. As I brought this information into me, I felt that I was becoming bigger, brighter, and more beautiful than I had ever felt in my life.

Pharaohtriea smiled at this, and then he asked me to turn the Bible over to the last chapter and read from the Book of Revelations. I did. When I had finished, he told me to read the second-to-last chapter. I did. He told me I was to begin again with the last chapter, read the second-to-last, and then read the third-to-last – and so on, all the way through to the beginning of the book. It came as a shock to me whilst reading, as I realized that I was seeing with new eyes and understanding the language of this journey of self-discovery, which so many of us are searching for. I had accepted this wisdom within myself, and, therefore, I felt that I had to become much more responsible for my own actions. I read those thousands of pages of the whole Bible in reverse order, and I finished the book in all its glory seven long years later. My heart opened up when I realized that the hidden language of Revelations was explaining to me how my body tuned in to becoming the unconscious mind.

The message became loud and clear: We must understand and accept our past in order for the future to prepare itself to appear before us. When we don't understand, we keep on creating another highway that we must walk, and then, if we take a look outside the front door, we notice that the whole of humanity is still repeating the same mistakes over again.

Humanity as a whole must accept the past in order for the future to be fostered within; this brings us closer into an alignment with the original source of God – or the Universal Laws. We cannot go against his "written word", which is scribed in every cell in your body. Years later, I found that the written word is our recorded genetic inheritance, which is embedded in every cell. As of yet, we are neither strong enough, nor capable enough, to understand ourselves, so how can we fully understand our own creation? When we return back into our own source, the freedom of self ignites the inner light, which releases an expanded version of our inner truth. Can you begin to accept the codes that were revealed and written in my previous stories regarding your self now? A ladder goes up and down, not sideways or inside out.

Many years have passed since that ETI, and I am still amazed at the hidden definitions of the codes in the Bible. I have introduced you to many stories from the Bible in this compendium of books, and I would like you to understand the gifts from God that are in your life right now. The Book of Romans explains it nicely in chapter 12, verse 2: "Do not be conformed of this world, but be transformed by the renewal of your mind." Further information is revealed in my eBook "Decoding the Revelations of Saint John the Divine".

The energy of Pharaohtriea stayed with me for the next ninety days; if I were to explain the truth regarding the wonderful experiences that I lived during that time, it would take me another 300 years to write it all down. My life was a miracle, moment by moment. I began to experience a deep feeling suffusing every cell in my body; I thought this was love for myself – and for the Higher Self – walking towards my heart. I felt I was the Egyptian God Thoth in the hieroglyph, holding the scales, weighing my heart with the feather, and knowing that they balance perfectly and are the same weight. The pain in my heart grew stronger as my confidence grew to understand and release all my previous experiences, all the pent-up emotions of my past that I had locked in through not knowing what to do. As time progressed, this feeling seemed to grow into a thunderous applause for who I could become; it became a source of strength and power that was releasing from the depths of my cells, as well as from my Soul. It was amazing to know that my wisdom of self was mirroring the Universal energy, and that we could relate to the oneness together.

My knowledge expanded, and I evolved into travelling through the cellular recognition of the body, where I could view the initiation of how we collect our thoughts and how they release to us through our dreams or later on, through our visions. I did not fully understand at the time, but I urged myself on, knowing that another step of understanding was on the horizon, and that, as I walked forward into my future, I would collect my inheritance. This is where the fear collects in those that have awakened to the ETI experience. A movie entitled "Fire in the Sky" explained this inner journey, through the pre-recorded story of a young man abducted for five days. Through his not understanding this mathematical inheritance, his fear blocked the energy and created barriers in lapses of time. This venture that he had awakened within himself caused him to live in torture throughout the walk into his unknown. Well, try years of this torture, not just five days! My poor ego was shredded to pieces, and yet I always knew that God had his arms surrounding me and was standing right beside me. And, through my trust and belief in what I portended to be God, I could realize the potentiality of the human mind. And also my Architect was there to explain to me what I hesitated to know.

As I grew into each story that he was explaining, I began to realize that I was travelling through my own bloodstream in minute form, releasing this inner information that we call our intelligence. As I traversed through these amazing life forms, I was given the biblical names of people and places that were mathematically applicable to these sacred codes. This alphabetical language was showing me the story that we must awaken within; the story of the people described in the Bible. I found that they were a coded recognition of this sacred language that was in relationship to all the parts of my body – blood vessels, glandular and nervous systems, muscles, tendons, bone tissue, and so on. I can tell you that, as I watched my wisdom expand and release itself, it shed an entirely different light on each subject. I came to realize that all these sacred temples that had manifested around the planet in many different cultures thousands of years ago were here as a blueprint for us to understand the truth of our inheritance – but they are also here as a blueprint for what we have the ability to evolve into. They were all explaining the same story. They are the coded recognition of the levels of our intelligences that we are able to inherit and use to our benefit.

Each morning at eight o'clock, we started work, and I learned to understand the higher codes of our mathematical intelligence. The next morning at six o'clock we would review the last twenty-two hours of work, just to make sure that I had understood it all correctly. After that, it was time for a power walk along the beach, followed by a shower to prepare for my lessons to begin again. In the beginning, I used the broom handle as my gym, and my body began to regenerate through my applying my mind to assess the weight to the handle and exercise my muscles. Within a couple of months, a new neighbour moved in next door – a gym instructor – and we began a program which strengthened my body to accompany the extensions of my mind. I began to grow not only intellectually, but physically as well. My skin was a wonder to behold; it came alive again. My frizzy hair began to straighten as I released this childish thinking that had previously created my stress. It became wavy and much easier to maintain. My atavism was beginning to reassemble itself, and I honestly felt connected to my ancient heritage. Oh boy! I gave myself a new name: "AskmeaquestionAndIwillgiveyoutheanswer!"

I came into contact with the earth's energies, and I found that I could absorb more information while the rest of you were sleeping. The interference of your dreams and thoughts that were being released through your astral bodies was no longer a hindrance to me. I loved to work with the energies that released after midnight. I learned to understand why so many of you could not get to sleep or were awakening through the night. Do you remember the stories that have been passed down of the training of the priests long ago, who were woken at midnight to attend their Matins – or was the word "Ma'at An's", which relates to the inner education through the opening of the heart ceremony? It all depended on your biological time clock as to why you woke at a certain time, and I found that your inner clock autonomically tunes in to the sun's waves of energy as it traverses throughout our time zones. The way that you digested your thinking, controlled this Divine instrument – or "clock". It had nothing at all to do with your age; it was the reliance on your energetic attitude towards yourself that created the tick of this "clock".

I also learned to understand the mental capability of self,

which is waiting for you in the wings of your own stage play. It is available for you to understand as you release and grow your own wings through opening your heart, which can only occur through strengthening your character into you accepting yourself. I had learned to create through me trusting a deeper relationship with myself!

Your Notes:

CHAPTER TWENTY ONE

Eleventh Dimensional Lessons

As the months rolled by, information filled me constantly, with each step always filtering through one after the other, as it all added to the value of my inner dictionary, which I now realized was part of the Collective.

One day, I was asked to prepare myself to move on from that area by the ocean; as my next place of importance emerged, I had to learn to detach from the place that had educated me and that I had grown to love. I allowed myself to accept the direction I received, which was to go out into the west to live on a cattle property – 540 square kilometres of beautiful land in the Australian Outback, four of the world's most wonderful people already living there. It was explained to me that I needed more estrangement and a deeper detachment from my family and friends, all of whom I remained constantly involved with. I knew that this attachment was through the last traces of my fear releasing themselves as a result of me still living and attached to my past thoughts, even though I did so much less now than ever before. I also knew that this would be the final step of my education, after which I would be able to bring all these new resonances together. And so I found myself living in a tin shed on the property that had been revealed to me; it was far enough away from the homestead that I could live and work in detachment, but not so far away that I was totally isolated from all of humanity.

The owner and caretakers of that land allowed me my stillness; they never once interfered. At first, they tried to understand where the dickens I was coming from, and they had immense difficulty accepting why I requested to live alone. They showed me respect, though, and that was what I needed most. The owner's family had been very good friends of my parents, and that helped. They soon became used to the lights moving about in the sky, and they were not afraid when I explained the phenomenon to them. One of the station-hands knew where I was in my worlds, as he was also at the beginning of his own quest, and so he explained his story to the others, and all was well. Thank you for your respect and courtesy, George.

The property is situated right on the Tropic of Capricorn. The owner was born on this land, and he had lived there for more than seventy years. He explained to me that the local Aborigines had lived on this land for thousands of years, and that this was a gathering place for the councils to meet, where they could bring their dreaming stories together. These Aborigines had taught him that, at a certain time of the year, the energy reversed the circular stones scattered around that area – not only did it move them backwards, but it did so three times. These sandstone balls averaged around 40 centimetres in circumference, and they seemed to pivot on the earth at their base. They were spherical, with a slight lump underneath their surface that supported them to revolve. Certain magnetic fields embedded in the area collected and came together to help create this miraculous phenomenon of energy.

One day, when I went out to the paddock to gather some of these stones to place around my shed, one of them fell off the back of the truck. When that stone hit the ground, a section broke away, revealing another layer of stone underneath; the same thing happened when a small piece broke off that second layer. All in all, this was three stones in one – with each layer wrapped inside the one that surrounded it, and it was a fascinating thing to see. Maybe if I had chipped the last stone I discovered, I would have found still another one embedded within! The energy of such phenomena is God – this **G**reatest **O**racle of the **D**ivine, the creator of these sacred Laws of the Universe that keep this planet – through rebalancing the magnetic fields in order to enhance the central vortex of the earth, all of which pays the piper and helps to keeps us and the planet aligned. Sounds ridiculous, doesn't it? Yet I had come to realize that every living species from under the earth to above the earth, also played their part in the same game.

When the occasional rains came, the powerful storms released from above were horrendous. The property was situated on a large seam of quartz, and, as the lightning struck the ground, the earth would be showered with sparks, and long blue streaks of electricity – around 30 to 40 centimetres high – would flash up into the sky from the ground. It was truly an amazing sight to see from the door of my shed. The energy released during the storms was electrifying, and I dared not walk outside.

These storms made me recall a poignant moment earlier in my life, which I will digress here for a moment to share with you. As I watched the lightning, I would remember the day that my husband asked my father for my hand in marriage. My father had walked around the table, bringing his reply together, and then he said, "Before I give my permission for this grand event, I have this to say to you: My daughter is never allowed out in a storm! If you can remember this, you will realize that it is a dedicated and responsible position that you have to uphold from now on, and I am very relieved to turn this over to you. Somehow, her body has these special energy spots, and she is attracted into creating static electricity." My husband never understood a word that my father had said – and my father could not explain it in a language that would please my husband's ego, although he remembered every word that my father had said to him that night, and he always watched me when the rains were coming. (I realize now that my father could release himself from his duties and pass over only when I had taken on this responsibility of mastering myself, many years later. He died only after he saw for himself how I had made my own Divine commitment and dedicated my life to be connected to the eternal source). There are many of us with the same difficulty walking the planet. Your turn will come, once you begin to realize the inner strength of your own state of mind.

Back to the story. When I first arrived on the property, I had difficulty learning to balance my body; I seemed to be constantly walking around in circles, and always in an anticlockwise direction. I realized that I was walking through Newton's Third Law of Motion. I felt like I had to push my energy into the earth in order to ground myself to walk straight ahead; thus, my body of light had great difficulties, in the beginning, learning to equate to these strange circumstances. It took me around three weeks to learn to walk without feeling like an astronaut trying to walk on the moon. I had to make sure my heels were planted firmly on the earth. I started to wear heavy boots, hoping that this would ground me, but it didn't work; the boots just pulled and cramped my legs!

My geomancy was so collective, it seemed to walk within me – I could feel the vibrations collecting above and all around me, as I was in the process of becoming my own perfect hologram. My journey into this realm began as soon as I arrived on the property, and then my movement into my eleventh-dimensional lessons began in earnest. I only had time to unpack my bags and make my bed. I found that I could read the earth as I was walking around, and I felt the energy trapped in pockets in the ground. Through the energy of the sandstone, I could recognize where the crystal quartz had placed itself; it even had its own taste. My geomancy began to explode through my mind – and I imploded through the cellular inheritance as well, where I could sense the vibrations, feeling like a decibel meter that registered the speed of each sound wave. I could sense an earthquake as far away as Mexico and India, and I could transcribe for others the velocity of its vibrations – I even knew how many people would die as a result of it, (also a code,) so that the rest of us could go on, given the opportunity to repair the damage that we busily created amongst ourselves in each moment.

One beautiful day, as I walked outside the shed, I began searching for a place to sit in the earth so that I could meditate in – my new teacher had asked me to bury my hips and the back of my legs in the soil, as this gave my body the opportunity to ground itself, where my gravity fields could realign with the Collective Consciousness. I had to learn to place myself into the stance of the Lord Buddha in order to open up the lungs of consciousness, which is in the area of the upper inner thighs. There is a reason for this, further into the book! I began to focus my intension around me, feeling a current of energy that ran under the ground beneath my right foot, and then moved over towards my left-hand side. It was a powerful energy, and, as I looked out to my left to see where it was going, I saw a spindly little sandalwood bush over in the paddock.

This tree was no more than 3 meters high, And I watched as the life force of the tree acknowledged me: The small tree began to quiver. Through the bright sunlight of the day, that quivering turned the tree into a vibration of bright silver, with iridescent pale green and flashes of gold – it was a sight to behold, that spindly little tree, standing alone in its new shimmering radiance amidst the red and brown colours of the desert. Instantly, I knew that my meditation spot was under that tree. The energy had introduced itself to me, and that spot became a favourite place to switch into my vision world, allowing myself to release and restore the vestibule that connected into my heart. The essence of the tree, when I attained my Buddha Consciousness, was pure bliss; I absorbed the tree's perfume into my own breath, which picked up this essence and released it into my cells. I picked up the tree's dead branches and tucked them underneath the seat in my car; when the heat of the day peaked, the essence in my car was magical. I also placed these twigs in my cupboards and draws. Thirty odd years further on, that same essence is still there.

Once I learned to find my way around these energy grids and got my head on straight, through learning to parry my thinking, I realized, I was in a finely-tuned state of mind; I just had to remember to remain focused and live in the moment, in order to maintain that state of mind.

It was at this time that I began to understand how our thinking collects and releases the Alchemy of the mind. I learned how our Alchemy relies on the thought that we manifest in each moment, also, that we each have the opportunity to collect the appropriate chemicals from within, for us to release up through the ascension of our own intelligence. This levitates our energy up into our concordance through the libraries of our cellular inheritance. This expediency creates a brand-new dictionary of words for us to always have on standby.

Your Notes:

CHAPTER TWENTY TWO

God Consciousness

Three light ships worked with me during my time in the desert. Those ships were the God Consciousness mirroring and reflecting back to me through my channels, letting me know that I was okay. They gave me the chance to discover my own discernment, where I could find the faith and courage to go on. I had to believe in those lessons; I needed to see a form of logical consciousness, and, if I went out too far, those lights gave me the confidence to come back into my reality. I had to expel through my own consciousness what a spaceship or UFO was, and how it built up its own sequences to move in a holographic manner throughout this planet. More explained further.

I learned to manifest time and move through my own future in order to see what I could create in a metaphor. I found that my body was evolving into geometric shapes, or beings; at first, I thought these from another planet, but they weren't – they were within my own aura. Those beings were reflections of my own thoughts, thinking in their emotional depth of time and reflecting back to me. This is what we refer to as a "time warp"'.

In humans, time warps through our own energies vibrating at a faster rate, which symbolically creates the strength for the ego to coincide with itself. When we do not understand this, it gathers back into itself and blocks our energy, which then becomes the next step of our fear, and we know that this is the forerunner to all our dis-eases. The inner realms give us the gift of achieving our reality. My totem power was coming alive.

I was like an astronaut shuddering through the gravity fields of the planet. Yes, we do that right here on the earth, as it introduces us to the fourth dimension. I seemed to be permanently going in and out of the G-Force – or fields of gravity – and I had to learn how to handle this in an upright position, with my feet firmly on the ground. I felt the deterioration in my bones, which, at times I thought were collapsing and breaking down. When I asked for help in understanding what I was creating for myself, I was told to rub and pull my legs back down to the toes, and then burp. This took quite a bit of practice, as it was not ladylike and went against the manners that I had been taught as a child. So back into another commitment to self I went, and I learned one of the most valuable lessons of my life. When we burp, we released the blocked energy that collects through supporting our fear. Now listen to this next piece of advice! When we burp, we release the negative energy that also surrounds a dis-ease. If the negative energy is released, what happens to the dis-ease? If its own life force has become depleted, it has no life force to feed on! Once I fully understood the importance of all this intelligence – and once my "beings of light" were satisfied that I had collected the codes to this exponential truth – the next lesson was placed before me.

My body began to puff up, and I realized that my gravitational fields were becoming heavier through my mind not being in attendance to my body, as the liquid in my cells began to gather and swell. In total, through this learning, I put on more than 40 kilograms in weight. I now realize why that had to be; I was out there searching in the cosmos, and no one was home! I was afraid of losing the intelligence that I had earned through living in the unconscious mind, so my fear had no substance to feed on. Remember that a fat cell has created itself through your mucus doubling back on itself! It becomes thick – all through a thought that you have previously had, that you have not taken the time to rectify and balance!

I was in my future, not connected to my past, and afraid to lose the moment. I had to slow down a bit, as my thinking had overstepped its mark; so the next lesson was to bring my body back into a format where I felt much more confident with my thinking. I had to remember to burp in order to release the energy that had busily collected itself.

When the flashes of light came back to me as confirmation of my thinking, I knew that I had to continue on until that part of the journey had completed itself. When I panicked, I rang and asked my teachers a question regarding my journey; I still needed confirmation on some of the answers. They could not explain these answers to me; their confirmation was, "You have been selected to complete this journey. Please go on; trust as you have done in the past, and remember that nothing can interfere with you, as you know that God is with and within you." I seemed to be walking over the deserts without water, climbing the sheerest mountains with shredded fingernails, and swimming the deepest oceans without pausing for breath – all from one side of the planet to the other. I felt that I was a pioneer, trekking the future for all mankind to view.

I was undertaking this strenuous journey of the underworld to know that I had to instil in me a belief that, when time had equated itself, all the truths would be revealed to me! Over the next few months, when my tears had dried and a veil of peace had seated itself within and around me, I knew that my confidence would become my strength and that it would sustain me. I said, "Thank you" many thousands of times, and then I picked myself up, dusted myself down, and began again.

Throughout this exalted time, I watched the manifestation of one of my thoughts, seeing how it collected in my mind and began to work all through evolving itself throughout my billions of cells to create that starship – or UFO. I watched how the inner light created itself, always starting at the lungs of our consciousness, our upper inner thighs; through the conductive electricity of my brain which freely passed throughout my nervous system. I watched as my thoughts changed, each one attracting the next. It was also interesting to see how my thoughts presented themselves in so many different shapes and sizes. Which one was important? Which one could rely on its self? Which one had to expand and grow in order to be able to sustain its self and not look for others to support it? I watched how the mathematics of the mind created the symbol, and then how that symbol changed as an emotion filtered through to form the next thought. I was watching how our consciousness created its own collective energy, which, in turn, created our reality.

I also learned that we never came from another planet; it is all happening right here on Planet Earth – or, "UR-T", which, through the codes, means "understanding and releasing the truth". We can take "UR-T" to the next level of consciousness and decode "EA-R-TH", which means "through my energy ascending, I release the truth from heaven".

These Beings of Light that presented themselves to me took on hideous shapes and sizes, at times; I still had to communicate with them, even though I sometimes felt that I was in the parking lot of a science fiction movie. I had to take note of the shape of their hands and feet, the shape of their heads, the warp in their spines, the way they walked, etc. Over time, I realized that they were vibrations of consciousness that had already evolved, that represented the emotional difficulties they had evolved into in order to digest what they were thinking. I was receiving their life force as to how they had continually gestated through their emotional upheaval of not understanding themselves. They were representing the genetic vibration that they had inherited. These same entities were also the personalities that all humans create within themselves, when the mind is out of balance.

I was learning to communicate with other species that had already evolved from the ocean (book 6- Dolphins); I discovered how they had prepared and earned their own evolution, through recording a balance to their understanding of what the Collective had relayed back to them. The majority of them were androgynous, through their positive behaviour evolving up into the unconscious mind. One of the most important species to me was the insect population; I understood that they read combustible energy through living totally in their evolution, which is equivalent to our unconscious mind. These were the worlds of the Extra-Terrestrial Consciousness; their hideous shapes and sizes were magnified through the awakening of my inner eye, as I received the creative reality that conducted their consciousness.

I was manifesting a large hologram, and I realized that I was working with the eternal energy. There were the faces of the stick creatures, the eyes of the fly, the head of the ant, and the blur of the wings of the cricket. I was living a re-enactment of the evolution of the human brain; this is the myth, which is one of the highest levels that create the largest facet of the geometry of the Universe. Those years of terror and anxiety all came together over the next few years, as I climbed out of the bottomless pit to discover that I had the sustainability to reverse everything that I had been taught. If I reversed everything, I could see how the manifestation had formed.

***

This is only a small percentage of what happened in my life at that time, as everything seemed to be shown to me in an instant. My mind had gone beyond its own value of time, and every lesson was given to me in the blink of an eye. I had to come back home into my body to release the energy, which allowed me to correctly seat all my information into my memory banks.

Our memory banks are a fascinating subject. Those of you still under the control of your ego – which, remember, is the mathematics of the left hemisphere of your brain – now have the opportunity to place in your internal larder at the back of the shelf, many experiences that are no longer of importance that have occurred throughout your life. Next time you rearrange your food cupboard, you will find that they have disappeared all by themselves! Your thoughts seemed to be rendered down through time. All of which is through the ego not having enough substance to hold onto the thought! This is filtered throughout your mind, through the energy conduited through the stimulation of the thymus gland. That is why it shrinks with age! Remember your ego can only feed itself off past experiences! This is why you still have a tendency to rely on others!

Those of us under the reins of our emotional worlds – which, remember, is the right hemisphere of the brain – remember the relationship of everything that has ever occurred. In my case, it is what has occurred to me; I am constantly reminding myself to do better, when I am exhorted by others. They announce to me what I could have done; it is as though I must appease their thinking in order to remember the freedom I have earned!

CHAPTER TWENTY THREE

Initial Contact

So many of you fear your contacts through the smell and taste in your mouth within your senses. I have listened to thousands of you around the world who wanted answers to your questions regarding the exposure of your initial contact. Many of you explained that you noticed that you were onboard a light ship, placed onto the operating table, where the torture began. Others of you remember the scenes replayed in the mind as to the cellular recognition of self, where you are placed into a ship with a huge interior, an emptiness that has no boundaries and seems to stretch for miles.

It is through this state of mind that we begin to notice the complex apartments which are layered storey upon storey; each room is like a cocoon or pod, and this is where you are placed to rebirth into your next state of awareness. You note that there are many others who are trapped in their own pods; some of them are just skeletal frames of people who have died.

Some pods are filled with the elderly, both male and female; others are young children or babies still wrapped in mucus, having yet to announce themselves to the world. These symbolic images are your thoughts – both those that have lived out their experiences and also those that have still yet to manifest. You have warped totally into your collective collaboration, where your cellular program is initiating you up into your unconscious mind. Now you can release all your fears regarding the ETI, as the correct information has been released to you.

Please allow me to explain to you that these pods are representing your personalities in different stages of transition; and a personality is a reflection of you that springs to attention to stand by you – to support you and to become a reference that you may use – in other words, they reflect and open the pages of the books that are in your inner library, referred to as your inner bible. Those experiences that are past their expiry date file themselves into your memory bank, where you have the ability to recall and use them as an example for future reference. You are seeing yourself through the minute formation which pertains to the eclectic vision that releases from the inner eye – or third eye.

When you have the confidence to nurture yourself with your new intelligence, you will automatically advance to the next level, where you release another layer and so on; all of which adds up to your "common sense"'. Remember that the word common is an area in a small town or village where one can find a respite for self. It is a gathering place where the villagers can collect and rejoice. I refer to it as a place where we can be happy and create festivals. It is much the same when you come into a vibration of Extra-Terrestrial activity – the chemicals autonomically alter in the brain in order to equate and rebalance your life. As you ascend up into the unconscious mind, you begin to smell and taste your own Alchemy. Your natural gases echo out from your own body, through your fear – now you can understand that it is your own odour that you smell, not the odour of the entity; its hologram is your own intellectual manifestation. The fear that you are suppressing urges your own chemicals to release on a higher vibration. Isn't it amazing that the power of just one of your thoughts can cause all the billions of cells in your body to dance to its tune?

Your Notes:

CHAPTER TWENTY FOUR

The Language Of Divination

I know that this next section is not going to impress many of you, and yet it is through my understanding of the language of divination that I have brought this together to explain it to you. It is time for me to continue to release this endowment of the mathematics that comes down from the Divine wisdom. I had to understand how our body reharmonizes itself through these elements of our own Alchemy climbing up into the latter strands of our DNA, which releases sulphur, helium, and other potent chemicals – even to similarities to the drugs that one uses for self to create a euphoric effect of detachment (i.e., marijuana, cocaine, and other oddities). As previously stated, some people who receive contact smell these harsh and astringent odours, which I have just explained to you as the fear that one creates in moments of extreme stress. Their own Alchemy had to reach a peak of perfection in order to initiate them back into their thinking.

Again, I had to learn to burp to release the pressure of condensed energy that I was collecting through absorbing the Collective Consciousness. I lived totally in my own world, busily focusing on every word that came into my mind. At that time, I was still reading the Bible backwards in order to understand the hidden language that had been heralded down to us in the first place. And remember, this intelligence was written in the coded language of Metaphysics, which, at that time, was so high that the priests spoke in parables (which, at that time, was still unknown to me, but which I now know as the "matter of physics").

I found that I had to have nerves of steel to support me, and I began to notice that, when I burped, I had this strong metallic taste in my mouth. As time went on, my intellect released, and my focus became stronger; I was living every thought to its completeness, and the tastes in my mouth changed drastically – helium, ether, anaesthesia, marijuana, and even advancing up into cocaine, where I experienced different euphoric effects for a few hours, until my mind became subdued as I finalized the end of the lesson at hand.

At that time, I thought I was overworked, and so God had given me a reprieve; at that basic understanding, I guess I was right – although that was not enough for me, and I needed to enquire more regarding this issue. I began to realize that this concise state of mind was where I fully understood the ancient pathways of the Shamanic resonance, where the Elders of the tribes took to the smoking ceremonies in order to travel through their veils and be delivered into a sense of euphoria; this was where they could escape from their ego, which could only survive in its own sense of reality. At that time my mind was focused on where I was receiving an uninterrupted eulogy, which was watching my thoughts working in parallels of geometry, in order for me to see how the original blueprints of different dis-eases created themselves and also how a cough, right down to how an orgasm had collected themselves. I was made aware of these elements as my mind took me into a sense of oblivion. My olfactory system had opened up beyond my conscious recognition of intellect, and this was where my senses had now become vibrant and alive; I watched as the odours automatically created their essence on my behalf. I smelt terrible – it was as though I was living inside the gas works – I had become a walking chemical plant. I came to realize that this was an achievement I had principally earned. And all this took place without experiencing any drugs at all!

Why do we victimize sports contenders, who have devoted themselves to a prowess of dedication through their discipline of self that strives and reaches up for an endowed sporting achievement, by testing their urine or blood for drugs? Many of you understand what I am talking about, as we have shared hours of talking around the table in many different lands, where you have spoken to me in your honesty to tell me that you had never taken drugs or solicited yourself to help you in your sporting endeavours and achievements. Over the years of dedication to your commitment, you had earned too much respect for yourselves. Do we still have to surmise and step away from something that we cannot understand, and will not accept, regarding our claim to self? If this explanation can be fully understood, maybe we can rearrange these laws that have been collected by those who are innocently still entangled in their unknown.

Throughout my training into understanding the inner language of the myth, it all began with the art of meditation. I came to realize how much quieter the mind became; the more focused the mind became, the more it began to add to, and open up to, the inner language embedded in our DNA – or, to use a later title, the "mathematics of the mind". Our mind, so we are told, is symbolically embedded with the last sixty-four generations of our family, which are the basic building blocks that create our intellect.

My training which began through the instigation from the tradition of the Tibetan monks, which we refer to as Esoteric Buddhism, and which is one of the oldest recorded forms of enlightenment known and explained to man. This form of meditation begins to add to our Divinity a state of clarity that we accomplish through focusing on ourselves.

During those twenty years of research, my fields in the underworld have led me into the power of just one thought. How do we create it? Where did it come from? How does it digest itself throughout our body to promote and make things happen for us? This led me deeper into understanding the Alchemy of the brain, which is what we refer to as the results of our inner library that connects us, as we learn to open up our mind to the hidden language of the unconscious mind.

My specialty in the pronunciation of thought comes through explaining to my students the autonomic responses of the unconscious mind. Once we start conducting our own thoughts, we are beginning to produce radio waves that the rest of the species of the planet also have the possibility of hearing. This we call "telepathic communication", which has been here since time began. As the recesses of my brain began to unwind, I could see through my dichotomy as to how my third eye – or inner eye – was searching my portals in order to create the concise alignment which would allow the next thought to release itself. Can you recall the stories of the elephants and whales, which have already evolved into this temperance? Who was King David? Which section of the body is he representing?

Now allow me to begin to explain to those dedicated people who have been declared guilty, but who know in their own hearts that they are innocent, that they are releasing this inner chemical that mirrors into the mathematics of the same mechanics that produces cocaine.

When people become addicted to relying on drugs, they are forcing their natural chemicals beyond their own belief. They have become outcasts to their own inner society. This releases the dopamine that the body naturally creates. And the more they depend on this drug, the more the dopamine reduces through their applying more cocaine for their inhibited use. There is no more natural pleasure in their life. They have moved beyond it, allowing their natural habitual feelings to coerce with their emotions. In other words, they have become self-centered, through depleting the art of creating their own happiness. They now have to rely on the chemical elements of cocaine to produce this euphoric feeling that gives them their enhancement.

The Egyptian mummies were supposedly cocaine addicts, according to the latest assumptions, as scientific technology has detected traces of cocaine in these ancient bodies. Therefore, the establishment has begun to question the intellect of these wonderful mummies, which are supposedly more than 3,000 years old. There are so many hieroglyphs with people who have the lotus flower in their hand and they seemed to be sniffing the essence. When we understand the divine interpretation we realize that they are absorbing the essence of their own soul, as this is what the water lily represents! Not a hallucinogenic drug!

Please allow me to explain this next part of the story to you. The higher our intelligence becomes, the more we equalize our mathematics. Those mummies were either learned scholars, or focused members of society, who had earned their mummification through their mathematics having reached a specified alignment; also, they were buried for thousands of years. Who is to say that we will not have the same chemical build-up in our bodies as we further our own intellect thousands of years hence? Those who still lived in their third-dimensional reality at that time had not earned this royal send-off to the next world.

Our mathematics are equivalent to the Collective Consciousness, which is the unconscious mind – our antenna climbs ever higher; hence, the symbolic spires on the top of churches. The more focused we become with our self as we advance our intellect, the more we automatically pull away from our childish thinking; therefore, the less we are likely to create excuses on our own behalf.

During my lectures, I noticed that, when I took my students into a meditation and their minds were quiet before they were introduced to the day's lessons, I became aware that my energy began to rise through the results of that large group of people focusing on themselves. I would start scanning the room, with my third eye, until I could begin to see the room starting to harmonize with all the colours of a rainbow. The more advanced the student, the more brightly they reflected the colours – especially when they had reached a state of harmony, where they became equalized to their own intellect. They had reached the antenna in their mind. This brought balance to their body, giving it the opportunity to repair and heal itself.

Those who were still learning to understand their curve of education were of a stronger and darker vibration. It is like the opening of the seven seals in the Book of Revelations, or the vibrations releasing from the seven chakras. I knew they were ready to continue when I had the whole audience tuning in to themselves. The euphoric state of mind naturally occurs, and the DNA releases and opens them up to waiting for their next enquiring thought. I could smell the odours that were releasing through their own endowment, and, when the room smelt of flowers, the students were ready to begin their education. Through their trust in me, they had entered up into their intellectual light to begin their next lesson. That same administration of quieting and refocusing their mind on themselves was echoing the same euphoric effect as cocaine. I found the students could open up their intelligence through understanding mathematically, how the DNA informs the brain to reinforce the Alchemy (the multitude of thoughts that they had earned) of their mind – that is, to release the next step of their intelligence.

For the students to accept the education of training to become a Shaman Initiate – which is spiritually a higher caste of human intelligence, and which is where we commit to our Soul's expansion – their stress and emotional upheaval became things of the past. They were patient with everything they chose to do, and they found that they could absorb all this extra knowledge through being moved out of their third-dimensional reality; also, they could enter into a space of silence and stillness, which drew them up into the language of the unconscious mind.

One of my mentors, Joseph Campbell, describes Shamanism as follows: "The Shaman is a person, male or female, who has an overwhelming psychological experience that turns him or her, totally inward. The whole unconscious opens up, and the Shaman falls into it." (Campbell, The Power of Myth, p. 86). Yes, the Shaman does fall into the unknown and through climbing up out of the bottomless pit (Revelations 9:1–2); we know that all is revealed at the right time, as my students had shown.

I found out, after many years of research, that it is the euphoric effect of dopamine, which we have spiritually termed "enlightenment", occur only when one has made a commitment to self. Do you hear this sentence? It was accomplished through years of my focusing on both hemispheres of the brain, which becomes the marriage at Cana-an, where Jesus turned the water into wine – where we receive a never-ending supply of support from the Higher Self. This is also an equation that some sports champions achieve through the antenna of their mind reaching the creation of the cocaine through entering up into their own mathematical memory, which is freely available to the expedient growth of one's own intelligence. It has nothing to do with physically taking the drug!

To this day, as I walk down the street or meet with others, I can smell their thoughts, and so I am immediately alerted as to how they are thinking; as a result, I am well prepared to know how to answer them. Your thoughts register with the Collective, and this sets your scene in motion. The freer your mind becomes, the more your odour, scent, or essence changes to reflect your thinking.

If I smell certain flowers, I know that your mind is on a learning curve. The smells of the flowers represent the different personalities you have tuned in to. If you smell of different odours through your thoughts, you were holding a bunch of flowers, I realize that you have opened many odours to collect your own freedom. I am impressed with this, all through you having climbed up another rung of your own ladder to create your future success. If you smell of herbs and spices, I realize that you have placed a tremendous effort into your education of accepting self.

If you smell of animal, I realize that your primal past is still caught up in a quandary regarding how you understand and accept your personalities of self. Also, the animal in you comes alive when you experience fear in your relationship with another person. The smell of cat, dog, fox, etc. connected to someone, shows me the levels of that person's attainment. The smell of animal faeces alerts me to a person who has held him/herself in abeyance to the past, having not yet found the courage to release the past and step out into the moment – and onward to the future. If your attention has not been focused on you – and if you cannot believe in you – you automatically hook into someone else who is creating the same excuses as you do. Like attracts like!

The smell of meat, for me, depends on whether it is chicken, lamb, beef, or pork/ham, as they all vibrate to a different frequency. The smell of salami is the worst, as it means you have minced your thoughts and are set out to destruct someone who offends you; your ego is so fired up with nowhere to go.

I came to my final conclusions at a business conference that I attended. I walked past a group of four of my colleagues who were just breaking up their conversation. As each one separated from the pack, their personal odours reeked out through their aura. I knew which one of them had placed their point of interest and was satisfied with the conversation amongst the others; I also knew who had not found the courage to speak out in reference to their own belief; and I knew which one of the group never paid attention to the conversation in the first place! Our odour can never lie; it is our Alchemy at work. It is another tool we can use through our truth releasing itself. As we travelled home, the subject came up in the car, and everything that I had thought in that moment was exactly the way it was in each person's reality.

During these heavy times, I noticed that I kept on wanting to change my clothes; the colours that I used to wear offended me now, and I reached for lighter colours. I craved white clothing – flowing, long, and loose.

Why? The discipline that it takes one to acquire and attain this state of consciousness is extremely strict and quite severe for the average human, who is still focused on others, as it is not yet their turn to focus inward. Each one of my thoughts had earned the choice of revaluing themselves, and colour became obtrusive to them!

Your Notes:

CHAPTER TWENTY FIVE

Pneumatic Waves Of Consciousness

My next advanced education began in earnest, in order to introduce me into the world of pneumatic waves of consciousness, which I already had begun to gather around me. Eventually these waves took on the shapes of people who appeared to walk through walls, one at a time, and then stand before me or sit on the bed beside me. To my state of mind, at that time, those people were complete in their holographic form, and they seemed real; as if they were physically there. I realized that I had intellectually entered into the light worlds – somewhere between matter and antimatter – so, again, I trusted these experiences, and I moved on.

One Soul who came to teach me had an aura of colourful energy that resonated around him for about 1.5 meters. Those brightly coloured energies sparkled and moved as he spoke. This fascinated me in the beginning, because, as he spoke his words, they never collided with the colours of the waves; the sounds and colours seemed to move in harmonic unison, as if their own movement reinforced them.

As this brightly coloured one came to the end of his conversation, more Beings of Light were attracted into my peripheral vision. It seemed that the next one was magnetically pulled towards me, and the one who had just finished was automatically pushed back. These incoming and outgoing auric energies travelled in a curve, seeming to circumnavigate the energy mathematically so as to determine in which direction to move. The polarity shifts of positive and negative were at work here, and I watched in continual fascination. I felt like a magnet that attracted these energies according to the resonation of the mathematics of my own emotional value at that time.

I realized that I was unfurling hidden dimensions that had been folded in on themselves since the time of my birth. My outer personalities, which I had used in regard to how I represented myself to others, as well as to what they thought of me, had protected these hidden realms. I had no interference from others out here in the bush, and the opportunity came for me to release my three-dimensional mind. I watched each released dimension multiply itself, which gave me a deeper insight to see from above – to extend my peripheral vision and to attract my future intelligence. Mathematically, my 3 x 3 had become 9 (to know the knowing).

Those threads of consciousness (or what is now explained in the language of physics as the "String Theory") seemed to be parallel worlds of me. They had become an added value to my future wisdom. I realized that my thoughts were the neutrinos that collected through these waves of consciousness to enter into those threads of information. It was as if they were memories released from the womb of the Universe. This ectoplasm of the Collective was gathering the information that I was to be reseeded with – all through the strength of my own thoughts searching for the right answer to one of my questions.

My body was pulled and stretched as I walked those worlds to enter into other recesses of my mind. My G-Force shuddered and warped through the waves that were echoing around me – until I could see my own colours harmonizing with one another, and then I knew that I had earned the right to go on. I have often related that experience to the story of Joseph and his coat of many colours. In the Arabic language, this is pronounced, "Your- Seph"; through the Metaphysical language, it interprets as "in your wings, waiting for you to collect your self". Remember, your wings birth once you have opened your heart to your self!

Those expressive Souls presented themselves to me as beings of young, middle, and advanced ages, both male and female; they came dressed from the past, present, and future. They represented all countries and spoke all languages. Whether they had beards or moustaches; were bald, or had hair parted in the middle, left, or right side, coloured black, brown, red, or blonde, and textured wavy, curly, or straight; had eyes of blue, brown, hazel, or green – they all were explaining to me the education I had earned of my own evolution. They wore shirts, skirts, slacks, shorts, jackets, and overcoats in patterns of florals, stripes, squares, and spots in every colour

– all of which contained symbolic messages for me as to what that personality was representing on the inside. The colours of their clothes and the designs on the fabric showed me where they were still caught up in the old dictionary of their mind. You are reflecting out to others, the garment you wear in your mind.

I had to learn that all of this was an expression of the exposure of the wisdom of the human mind. Those stories were explaining to me how we created our emotions and how, through our acceptance of self and our body language, we became a greater and more learned species. I learned to read everyone who lived in my earthly domain; I could see their emotional and egotistical thoughts exposing themselves for all to view. My third eye was so magnified that I could see all the games or excuses that we try to play with our own mind – and also, the games and excuses that we try to force upon others when we are in doubt.

Sometimes those Souls would walk through the wall with overcoats on; they would not speak to me, but we would play charades in silence. I had to guess their emotion of the moment, creating a story about what they were thinking, – first, through their shape and the colour of their hair; and then, through the clothes that they had on beneath the overcoat. For example, what was their thinking when they wore a blue and grey striped T-shirt? What was the difference between stripes and patterns? What were they asking their unconscious mind for? What did they want to achieve? How would these clothes get them to where they expected an outcome? What were the results that they could achieve by means of the garments they wore?

I had to learn to understand the nurturing of the human mind in its completeness before the next journey could be revealed to me. This went on twenty-four hours a day, month after month; and, eventually, I began to realize that we were here to play this game of human involvement in order for us to attain and feel complete. Once it had completed itself, and the education was over, I realized that I had been trained to see how the body waves were, "arking" up into the brain, which explains the story of Noah's Ark in the Bible. I had been delivered back to Babylon!

My next awakening was when I began quoting words of Einstein as they presented themselves to me; I noticed that I had been given his theories of relativity, which is how our body earns its own gravity fields in order to keep our feet on the ground and our head in the air!

Please point yourself in your own direction in order to have the confidence to create your field of space in the Universe; this is where you become at one with the Collective.

I also began to realize why I had to be alone out there in the desert; I would not have been able to take on this responsibility with others around me. I had to accept my interpretation of those famous biblical words, "I Am that I Am."

Your Notes:

CHAPTER TWENTY SIX

The Worlds Of Holographic Imprint

The same stories I am relating here at this time, are also explained to us in the Bible. When you understand the Bible metaphysically, Daniel, Ezekiel, Isaiah, and John – to name but a few – will explain to you all about light ships. The time when they spoke and released the inner language was thousands of years ago, and it was through their visions of what they had earned. Our inheritance all began with the stories of mythology (my theology - my way of life, or my religion, from the Latin language, religio - linking you back to the source).

This indelible imprint of holographic importance is seeded throughout every human. You are the Extra-Terrestrial Intelligence; you are the Alien, and also those Star Beings or Beings of Light. It is the inner workings of the human brain – or the Arcing of the Covenant – which is the unconscious mind reflecting back home to God.

These worlds of holographic imprint affect each of you differently, according to your own growth of intelligence. For example, three people in three different vehicles see an accident happen, and yet, if they each have their attention focused on themselves, they will see three different versions of that accident. Their Divinity is in a different scope of Intelligence. Another car with three people inside saw the same accident, although, these three had been communicating with one another regarding an issue, and so their thoughts were focused on the same subject; they had become one mind, and so they all saw exactly the same scene. They were all on the same wave level, as they were all living the same experience. Their interpretation may have differed slightly through their explanations – and/or through one or more of them being more advanced intellectually into their own wisdom.

Once I understood all this information, I realized that I had been shown the physics of the human form. I had formed a complete relationship with myself! And the higher we fly in the mind, the less our judgment of others is portrayed in our mind. We are all one, no matter what our religion or way of life is.

We are here to learn to understand the mathematics – or "Ma'at-He-Ma'at–Ic's" – of the Universe. Can you see the coherent energy in this? What does it do to you? The word mathematics automatically – or should that be "auto-Ma'at-ically? – creates energy to move forward through its own motion, from our solar plexus region up into the heart area, and continuing on to connect with the brain. The relationship to the Collective is created through the codes of the language coming together.

I have assessed many intellectually disabled patients regarding the instability of their inner intelligence. They each had a story to unfold, according to how they saw it, and I had been taught over many years to understand their story. They were not unbalanced in their mind; they spoke about what they understood, and what they had seen through their own level of intellectual understanding; in other words, they just relayed the parable that they were receiving. The rest of us must learn to more clearly understand the mental transmission that these people receive. It all depended on how they touched their body; that is, where their fingers began to explain their telepathic inheritance. Every one of us touches our eyes, our ears, and our face, or scratches our arms or legs, etc.; but how many of us understand that these movements are reflecting the hidden language? This is how the Collective answers metaphysically – or, to look at this another way, it is the telepathic communication from the Higher Self, but the intellectually disabled do not know how to understand or interpret the language that is passed down to them from their own "Divine Will".

The important question is: How do we learn to understand them? This is a lesson we must learn. The answer is that all returns to us through the movements of their arms and legs, where they touch their body and/ or facial features – the part of their eyes that they touched, the upper or lower lip, the part of their ears that they touched – whatever it is, we must determine whether it was a positive movement or a negative reaction. Why did they scratch that spot of their arm, and was it the lower section or the upper section? What was their Soul – or unconscious mind – trying to inform us regarding their thoughts? This is the unconscious recognition of their self answering back to us through the thoughts that we have in our own mind! Ask the question, and they return their answer! This is the sacred body language at work, hopefully my next book.

If you try to follow the next paragraph, you will gain an understanding about what we receive when Beings of Light (or other higher forms of energy) transform their energy into ours. This next paragraph is a typical transmission that I reached up into the Collective to receive.

The language of mathematics is the hypotenuse of the contradiction. It announces itself as the two columns of the DNA, to the two brains, which reverberate to square. This equates to the solitude of perspective recognition. We, therefore, claim our magnitude to all that is by focusing our recognition on current values of time, space, and matter. The energy then equates to the building frames of the perpendicular motion of the DNA, which pulses into our intelligence through our glandular system. This magnitude and solitude represent a cluster of globules that enhance the proteins that protect the DNA. The liaison of the abstractive is a conjoining of collective recognition which promotes the ionization of gravitational force.

All that information is in connection with the DNA. How many of you can understand the seriousness of the channel? That transmission came when I was working on my book "Decoding Disease", and if I would have written the book in that language, not too many of you would have understood what I was saying. I then had to learn to understand just what I had received and it took time – time and a half, really – for me to equate the messages back into a language that you could all understand. Slowly, the information unravels in the brain so that it may be understood. Once we have tuned in to understanding our wisdom, the answer will automatically come through when it is needed to express a pronunciation of an intension that the planet is searching for. The Collective

Consciousness places the transmission in front of us, through each step advancing on itself, one at a time.

As you start to experience your intellectual flow, you will begin to open up your vision world, and then you will be able to see a dream unfolding for you to understand while you are awake. You are looking at the invisible, through the world of the Metaphysical – you are looking between the lines, not at them! Some people call this daydreaming! As you expand your consciousness further, you will begin to see the dream playing its role in front of you, explaining your truth of the moment by reflecting it back to you.

When we dream while we sleep, many of us cannot remember those dreams when we awake, as we are blocked subconsciously. Our ego – or our fear, or primal/conscious mind (all these are the same!) – sits on top of our emotions when it is being tested to open up its excuses, and it rests only when we are asleep. This is connected to the energy of the hypothalamus area. While we dream, when our ego is still, it allows our subconscious to report to our unconscious mind, which then communicates back to us on an esoteric, not an exoteric, level. The hypothalamus section of the brain is your world of control, but the control that you have over yourself inhibits your understanding.

Visions are released back to you through many levels, and, as you evolve into this program, you will receive different interpretations as to what your own collective is announcing to you. You expand your wisdom as your intellect evolves. I call the hypothalamus the "last hurdle that we jump through" in the third dimension of our reality – that is, before we step up into the doorway of the unconscious mind. That relaxation period when you are asleep is where you and God are one; this is when you are ready to hear the voice of the prophet within.

The journey within is the story of myth and legend. We began our lives through listening to those stories, and they automatically relaxed our fear throughout our childhood. While someone else told us his/her story, the responsibility then became theirs, not ours. We were able to use this fractional response for our own strength to abide by. If you respect yourself while you are living your life – if you are not afraid of responsibility – your fear, through accepting its own wisdom, can freely release its bondage, which has controlled you for most of your life.

The myth is the magic of the aura, it is where our evolution is stored. Through not believing in self, we automatically try to control others. Remember that the word control means "the confusion of the troll within us". That troll is known by many names – the Beast, the Devil, the Dragon within, etc. The troll – or the controller – is the little person with a small mind that is trapped inside. He represents our fear, and, because that little mind will not release its hold over itself, it spends its life trying to control others. We see the troll in all his glory at the entrance into the Vatican.

Remember that the definitions of this planet are an illusion, looking at the illusion, creating the illusion, collecting the illusion, for the illusion. No matter what happens in your life, it is all meant to be at that given time; it must happen to you just as it happens – until you become that end illusion that you are so busily creating, all by yourself. That final illusion is your "Vision World" – or your "Vision Quest" – it is where you become the source of your own knowing. It is only four little words, which, through the codes, interpret as, "your truth releases through understanding your Soul".

In order for you to manifest your future, you learn to become the illusion of self. You automatically become that outer auric field; all of which creates a vibration that collects your future on your behalf. The more we become that permanent mirror – or outer boundary of self – the higher we extend our intellect; that boundary is the light of your own creation, which is urged up to become the cap on your pyramid. It is the outer boundary that collects your strength. It must equalize with your inner thoughts.

How do we become our own illusion? We have learned that our left brain is our ego, and our right brain is our emotions, according to the sacred language. This has been explained to me through my understanding of the hidden codes of the Bible, which was written in a language explaining the evolution of our unconscious mind. We train our ego to look at our emotions, and, in return, those emotions mirror back to us. When we understand all this information, the autonomic responses of our nervous system help to ascend us to the next level. This governing of self is what we are all about – it is not the two brains melding, rather, it is the two separate entities walking the same path. The illusion is created through the equality of both brains walking hand-in-hand with one another, which then becomes our intellectual light.

Both brains evolve to a certain level, where each can view the other in balance; at that point, the reflection begins to manifest. This then becomes known in the beginning as the Higher Self – or the "Royal Order" of things to come. That order is what we refer to as our "Godhead", and this is where we open ourselves up into the pineal gland. Through our thoughts coming together, we balance our energy, where our light becomes the reflection of the two hemispheres of our brain. The Higher Self is what God has freed from the ego's restrictions, as it learns to harmonically balance and extend itself. As we reach up, we find that we are able to look down at the same time. Goodness! I hope you understood this paragraph. Please read it again. I will explain to you another reference, and also remind you of the section inside the brain where the last hymen of the five virgin births was shredded, metaphysically speaking; I am referring to the pineal gland, that sacred area that is also known to us as the "Eye of God".

A reflection creates an image, and an image is something that we have created through balancing the illusion of self. For example, we can put different lenses on a camera in order to create different images. It is exactly the same with our mind as we intellectually evolve ourselves. We create a wonderful multifaceted hologram of self, and that hologram is the result of our thinking. An illusion is something that automatically builds and creates itself through the light that we manifest, and the result of that illusion becomes our reflection.

A "facet" of you is one of your personalities that has reached its own attainment. Allow it to forge itself into its own brightness. Make your facets sparkle and shimmer with the light and the brightness of a diamond. What a gift we had on this planet when Sir Isaac Newton released his wisdom! Once you have created that facet, you cannot go back and rest on your laurels; in order to keep that diamond balanced and bright, you have to equalize all other facets to the original – this is the permanence of light. Please look for the clear light within you! You are supplying the light for others to see through their heart in order to exalt themselves. I am metaphorically explaining the mythical story of the lesser Gods.

Remember the colours we read of in the Bible describing Solomon's Temple; these are the colours created through the last of our royal glands arching and opening up to accept their own responsibility – that is, to create our rainbow. As each of the seven seals are opened, they release their harmonic colour, which then blends up into the pineal gland. Through the parabolic effect, the four glands that create the parathyroid area arch their way up through the glands of the lower brain, where they reconnect to the pyramidal section that houses the medulla oblongata. We can understand how each crown has the arches crossing over to keep the crown balanced. These colours become the jewels of our crown; this is what royalty wears on solemn occasions to show us, symbolically, how our intellect announces itself.

I remember my soldier husband using spit and polish on the toecaps and heels of his boots before going on parade; it took hours of his time to bring forth that shine through his own accomplishment. The cloth had to be the softest one could find. It is the cut and polish that creates the sparkle of the diamond, not the diamond itself, which is merely an illusion of its own worth. If that diamond is in all its clarity once it has been centered, it will create and pronounce its own magnificence through its reflection of itself!

This effort places intelligence into your consciousness; it shines through you, and it is where your Soul becomes free and learns to walk on the outside of your body. This is when every cell that you awaken allows the light to compound and expand. As that light expands, it releases your inner knowledge; it adds balance, and, in return, it harmonizes itself. This is when you become balanced in the mind – as you think, so it must be; and, as you earn, so it will become! Now do you understand the importance of your outer boundaries? Be careful what you ask for – you just might receive it!

When you use your Soul energy with intelligence, it is called "emotional intelligence", which becomes your Spiritual Inheritance. Through your own confidence, you will reflect yourself back to you. Stand tall when you speak to others! You are emitting something that they have not yet released in themselves. Your intellectual light will introduce them to their own pathway.

Your Notes:

CHAPTER TWENTY SEVEN

Releasing The Divinity Within You

What you are thinking in this moment is automatically ("automa'atically") being programmed for the next generation of humanity. You are programming your children, grandchildren, and their children's children. You work on the level of cause and effect – that is, until you begin to understand what the effect of the cause is.

As you birth the next generation of your family, you automatically place the responsibility of your fears and joys onto them; thus, the sooner you eradicate your negative responsibilities and improve your own intelligence, the sooner your children are allowed to be free to take the family's lineage to a greater height. That is how the Extra-Terrestrials – or Beings of Light – explained to me why we humans keep on repeating the same mistakes, creating greater difficulties for our children as they try to exalt themselves into their future embedment, where they can create a greater society for every human to view.

The ETs also explained that the only war should be the one going on inside us, as we learn to harmonize our own mind; it should not ever be given back as a confrontation to another human. The word war, through the codes, means "our wisdom ascending and releasing". No fewer than 128 wars are happening continuously around the planet, in many different lands, every day. Again, we see the codes at work. We have created this number unconsciously, through not advancing our thoughts; and so, to our detriment, as one war finishes another one is created. Also, to add to this information, is our realization that it takes twenty-eight years for a war to collectively build and create itself for it to manifest and then run its own course. Of course, that gives us the equation: $4 \times 7 = 28$. We are busily creating these codes to stay with us for our future generations to uphold. When will we see the Collective Consciousness balance itself and change the number of these codes? Is this humanity's progress? We have not yet earned the intellectual right to fight our fellow man!

At this time in our evolution, we have put war into the "too hard basket", as it is an easy way out, in the moment; one day, we will have to accept more responsibility for our thinking, and not send our fear out to be carried by others. If you cared to read the Bible again with this new understanding of the hidden agenda, you would receive a totally different picture as to what was written and how the Elders of the tribes who have walked before us interpreted the original story back to us. Do you honestly think that these Prophets who wrote and collected these stories were interpreting that God said, "Let there be war, and there was"; or, were his words, "Let us go out and kill one another to save our own face or to protect the mask we hide behind!" Did he then add as an afterthought, "Oh! Please don't forget to love one another, while your thinking is in such a progressive behaviour." God is a pure inner light that is impregnated into every cell of every human; this light also communicates with every cell in your body, as it is the energy of humanity. This light is available to each of us, twenty-four hours a day! If only you could learn to listen to your Higher Self, you could hear God communicate through your inner realm to you – that is, your outer self.

You create what you think, and, as you think, your energy goes out into the Collective Consciousness, where it forms its own life force. That life force must go somewhere; if you do not take responsibility for yourself, it must be reflected to the next person who thinks just like you do. Remember that the dark and light forces are equal – it is not a war between the two – it is the acceptance of each that releases our free will.

You are responsible for each one of your thoughts, so your journey on this planet is to take control of your thinking and learn to become your own Law of Self, which, in turn, connects to the Universal Laws. You can heal the planet and clear the Karma of humanity; but, you can only achieve this once you have healed yourself! Healing yourself gives your children the freedom to evolve their own life program, which are those books in their inner library that they birth for themselves, through their own gestation.

Your genetic make-up, symbolically, is the last sixty-four generations of your family; however, in order to go forward on your educated journey of life, you must also go back through those genetics to release their trauma. As your knowledge grows, the more understanding you release and expand within yourself, which will automatically clear the knowledge of past generations. As you pull yourselves up into a higher form of acceptance, you will change that frequency, and that is how the Law of Self maintains itself.

You have the ability to eradicate Karma – or the cause of your actions – from the next sixty-four generations of your family; all you have to do is ask yourself what you need to learn and understand right now. Yes, it is that simple! That clears the pathway not only for yourself but also for your children and your children's children, as already mentioned. Once you have accepted that knowledge and are willing to move towards releasing the Divinity within you, the God within and you become one.

This intellectual pathway tears away all your old beliefs; for, through understanding those beliefs, you learn how you can allow irrational emotions to subside. Do not allow your old thinking to rule! Instead, allow your insecurity of self to relax and abate, so that you can step up into your next level of intelligence, and your new thinking can reign supreme.

We tend to grab a thought and hold onto it when we cannot find an immediate answer; by holding onto that thought, we forget about the rest of the thoughts that are all caught up in that one emotion. They have to be placed somewhere! Your ego or left brain creates this darkness, so you must bring yourself into a balance in order to view that darkness without either emotion or ego; this balance, in turn, promotes your light. Learn to believe and trust in yourself and through this accomplishment, and then your darkness will have the opportunity to dissolve. In other words, as your light shines, you learn to master yourself.

When a problem presents itself, please remember that you are in control; do not allow that problem to be in control of you. If the problem is in control of you, do not try to overpower it. We tend to place ourselves into a fixed energy, where we say, "I can beat this!" – but that is not right. Fixing a problem is not about trying to beat it; it is about looking at it in order to understand how and why it created itself. Once you understand the problem and the source of its creation, that problem will have the opportunity to find its own strength, and then it can reseat itself. Through the mathematics of the realignment of self, the problem will autonomically diminish into the ether. You are not here to defend yourself; you are here to release the freedom that you have sublimely inherited. It is not whether you win or lose; it is how you exalt yourself into participating in the game.

Your Notes:

CHAPTER TWENTY EIGHT

The Five Steps To Birth Your Godhead

Allow me to digress here. The pineal gland embedded in the centre of the brain has a hymen (membrane) layered over it. This is in relationship to the explanation of the five virgin births previously mentioned. It all began with the writing on the walls of Egypt, where the hieroglyphs described the five free days that each human could create in one year. Throughout the Egyptian principles, a year means a lifetime. We have been taught that a year is twelve months. As we exalt intellectually up through our layers, our language changes, and we note that a year is represented as a lifetime. To equalize this information with the unconscious language, we can bring this into today's equation, where we are explaining a lifetime, as just one of your thoughts. These five free days were a gift from the Rha, and these codes were carried forward into Christianity and changed into the five virgin births. Those five virgin births begin to give way as we release our Divine intellect, which becomes our telepathic behaviour that, in turn, supports us up into the unconscious recognition of self. Do you recall in my book "Decoding Sexuality and Spirituality", where I explain my theories as to how a woman collects and creates her own orgasm? Five energies must coincide with one another inside the vagina, and they eclectically inherit themselves through the glands, right up to the pineal gland. Through a woman yearning for her own fulfilment, she must collect her feelings up into these five areas in order for the orgasm to reanoint with the clitoris.

So, too, it is throughout this next education of life. We find that five glands are protected with a hymen (membrane), and as our intelligence unfolds, we shred the hymen from each of those glands, through accepting the new knowledge that is placed before us. It is an autonomic pronouncement heralded down through our central nervous system.

We begin with the thymus gland, where we learn to be truthful to our self; this is the myth of opening up our heart to reveal the inner architect known as Thoth, who held the scales to weigh the feather with the heart, through the writing on the walls in Egypt. This is represented by the cough – that is, through your inner thoughts reminding you of something you need to say that you do not say, you cough! In other words, you are swallowing words that your mind feels the need to release. To shred this hymen may take a few months; it must learn how to trust in itself, as it has been closed down through many generations.

In order to reveal your truth, you must next shred the hymen protecting the thyroid gland, which upholds our thoughts in order to release the confidence we need to speak our truth. It is the explanation of the opening of the mouth ceremony – again, through our understanding of the Egyptian philosophies. This is the final announcement for the ego to realize that it cannot turn back to return to its old ways. It has entered up to the doorway of the Divine Energy of the unconscious mind, where the third-dimensional reality is held in abeyance, in order to become a reflection of its intellectual light for others to follow.

The next step is opening the door to release the hymen from the hypothalamus gland, where the twelve strands of our DNA – or biblical Disciples – have earned their freedom through entering into the medulla oblongata in order to become our Divine support team. We have stepped up into our own space station, where no thought can interfere with, or interrupt, our spoken word. Remember, this is the area of the brain where the Beast (our fear is still trapped in our ego) is released!

From here we enter into the statehood of our pituitary gland; we understand the responsibility this gland represents, as it has to equate each thought and bring it into its own wisdom, where we head our own justice department, as we evolve deeper into the Divine equation.

The fifth and last one, of course, is the pineal gland – which is also called the third eye or the "Eye of Horus"; this is where we see everything from above. We have now entered up into the Akashic Records in order to reveal the secrets; this is where we are free to personify ourselves through the personal communication we have with the Sun God Rah, who represents the Eye of God.

May I repeat this previous paragraph and inform you once again that, through the codes of the unconscious mind, the pineal gland is the fifth virgin to birth. It has an eye at the top of the gland, which we call the "Eye of Horus" (also known as the third eye or the eye of the Godhead). Through the Egyptian philosophies, these are the five free days granted to us once we have earned these levels of truth. We have symbolically become the Hieroglyphic Empire. Or, if we look at it through a Greek mythological legend, it is symbolically presenting to us an explanation of the life of Cyclops. That eye can only look up; it cannot look out, down, backwards, or forward.

When you have birthed your Godhead – or your Eye of God – you have achieved your life's force, not the force of your life. That you had to accomplish to get here! When that eye has opened, you have achieved everlasting life. So, as you can see, even we have the chance to create our own concubines.

Your Notes:

CHAPTER TWENTY NINE

Pharaoh Of Your Own Land

During my completion of my Shamanic education and training, I learned to earn the sacred path of non-attachment. This gave me the inner strength to be open to the Collective Energy that the Universe had delivered to me. I began like the old party line on the telephone, where anyone could hook into any conversation. This occurred during those 120 days of trance that I spoke about previously. I could not pull myself out of that exposure of the unconscious mind, and, ever since that time, I have not really wanted to. My "big bang" had occurred!

At first I went into a heavy trance, where I could not remember what I had said, and I was very frightened of being in that state of mind. I thought I was having seizures, as I had great difficulty in controlling the twisting of my body. My cry to God was, "Please stand by me! I have no control over what is happening. I have to place my trust in someone, and you seem to be the only one who I think is listening." After three hellish days of stumbling around my home, the seizures began to abate.

After a while, I began to remember what had been said, and, through time passing, I grew to trust in all – and my self-confidence grew along with that trust. I now know that the Universe is mathematically positive in its repetition of mirroring itself. I also know that my energy is, too, as I have educated myself in that way. "Who is giving me this information to me?" is a question I no longer ask, as the answer no longer interests me.

The only channel that gave me his name was Pharaohtriea – or, as I first understood his name to be, "Fa-ra-o-tri-EA". Why? It was the only one I asked! The others I felt were intrinsic parts of myself that had collected through my previous generations. But, when it came to aliens, I needed a little more confirmation! It took me another nine years to understand the meaning of that name. I had been invited to Germany to give a series of lectures on the "Language of the Body", and also to explain my version of the Collective, and I needed to find an interpreter who could speak – and, hopefully, understand – my words. In the beginning, many came and went, as they had great difficulty in keeping up with my status quo; my energy was too strong for them to keep up with my words. I never realized how severely the intensity of the intellectual light could handicap the uninitiated mind. I thank every one of those beautiful people for striving to keep up with my stories.

A woman called Eva appeared in my life, and she found her own tremendous courage to keep up with my language – and with me – she did a magnificent job. I had already earned the right to open up my Universal language – where I could be given an immediate response to what they were saying in the German language, and have it promoted back to me in my own native – thus, I could fully understand Eva as she repeated my words in German. Someone in the seminar asked, "Who is your channel?" As I introduced my channel's name to the group, Eva repeated the name as, "Pharaoh Tri-EA". "No! No!" I interrupted her, "That is not the name." "Yes, that is your word interpreted into the German language," she said. Lo and behold, I realized that I had been trained all along to go to Europe and explain the hidden language. Even my Higher Self had hoodwinked me!

We all know what a Pharaoh is; "tri" is the three, and "EA" we know is the last God that we release from ourselves. The Collective Inheritance of the name Pharaohtrica is: "the Pharaoh who has collected and earned the three minds of God".

All these years of training were now coming into fruition, and I could explain the story of why the Pyramids and great temples of Egypt had to be placed on the planet exactly where they are.

Remember, there is never a mistake! I understand now where we collected and created the name of the word tree, as that is what the tree species are explaining to us – they have evolved from the seed of gestation to become the Mind of God.

This is how the Collective Consciousness explains itself. The codes of Collective Energy become the languages of our emotional worlds. They do not represent any one thing; they represent everything we say and do! My excitement grew as I had confirmation of these codes that automatically set themselves into the consciousness of the person who speaks, depending on how he/she unfolds and hears his/her own intelligence! We each become the Pharaoh of our own land! Wow! Aren't you magnificent?

Your Notes

CHAPTER THIRTY

The Afterlife

Over time, many people have taken an interest in searching for the tombs of the Pharaohs; as a result, many countries contributed financially to this endeavour, sending the right people who could offer their educated assistance on such excursions. None of them failed; they all applied their intuition and brought forth a reminder of the hidden language – or the Universal language – that the Egyptians had left us.

In 1922, the responsibility fell on the shoulders of Howard Carter, whose sponsor, Lord Carnarvon of England, released a tremendous amount of money in support of this endeavour; they were just about to abort the digs when a tomb was unearthed. Not just any tomb – Carter unearthed the tomb of Tutankhamen. When the world learned of their find, it created a "Tut" mania.

We note that King Tutankhamen's sarcophagus was created in three stages; the first two were made of wood and rolled in gold leaf, and the third was made of solid gold. Also the design of the sarcophagus is created in the unconscious recognition of the Asian language, as St John the Divine was explaining to us in the Book of Revelations. We must release the first God "EL" in order to allow the second God "AN" to further educate us into releasing the relationship of self – that is, into becoming the third God "EA", as explained to us through the myths.

The rich treasures were brought to the surface, catalogued, and transported to museums, where they were documented even further. Each item in those tombs was a code of emotions designed to carry the young mind of the Pharaoh through to the next step of his journey – or, as we have been taught to call it, to the "afterlife". The findings that fascinated me the most were the "Shawabti" that were found in the tomb; these included the figurines that represented one personality for each day of the year, as well as a group of thirty-six figures that represented each of the twelve strands of the DNA in triplicate – one set for each of the three layers of God ("EL", "AN", and "EA"). I think that the whole tomb is the combined wisdom of our own personal toolbox, which we keep with us as we journey through the discovery of our self!

We do not have to die physically to reach the afterlife. All it means is that we have reached a zenith of one stage of our intellectual life, and, thus, have earned the choice – or been given the chance – to evolve up to the next advanced stage of our Spiritual life. Remember, your Spiritual life is how you think to do!

We can now accept how the myths and biblical stories evolved, passed down from generation to generation, through the language of the Elders who wrote them. Those Elders were the Sages, Prophets, and Scribes. We each are given our own personal riddle at birth, and our journey is to evolve our intellect up into the spheres of telepathic communication; throughout our life, when the ego is in its own repose while we sleep, our dreams begin to inform us through this hidden language. The afterlife, when understood correctly, is the opportunity where we all release ourselves up and into the next phase of humanity's earnings. I bid you welcome to the secret codes that expose the language of Metaphysics. The Gift we were left to go on with is known to us as the Ark of the Covenant. As we release our intellect, we automatically ark ourselves up through those three Gods to become our own Ark. The knower of ways! It has been securely closeted within us forever, and the only way you will find it is through you discovering you. You own it! You are it! It is your brain that returns your thoughts back to you, through your central nervous system, and it will continue to communicate with you through the language of the unconscious mind.

Tutankhamen supposedly married his sister, and she supposedly lost two children who were near birthing age. That, again, must be understood correctly. Metaphorically, it is the story of our wisdom releasing, through the left and right hemispheres of our brain, marrying to form a relationship with one another, which promotes within us the opportunity to move up into the unconscious/higher mind. Again, I am explaining to you the biblical marriage at Cana-an, where the water was turned into wine.

The code is on the Golden Throne with the blue headwear of both male and female, which represents the royalty of the mind. All mythical stories from each land herald the colour blue, which relates to the "royal" approach as we enter up into the unconscious mind, where we learn to speak only through the opening of the mouth ceremony we have earned; this is where we become the mouth of the heavenly realms. Remember that the Blue Lotus depicted in many hieroglyphs is explaining the royal behaviour we earn as we journey through the memories embedded in our Soul. Another version is the Blue Buddha, who birthed through the lotus, as foretold throughout the Indian empire.

The two female children placed in their own sarcophagi beside Tut represented to us the emotional value that the boy-king had acclaimed through the concise education that enabled him to become a total enlightened being. Therefore, these babies had nothing to inherit. One is depicted as seven to nine months of age. What is the number nine (9)? The child had mirrored her own gestational period! Nine also symbolizes death, through the knowing of all. The other child had not yet proclaimed her own origin. To explain through the symbolism of the codes, they could not live on – again, they had no place because Tut had already earned his place in the eternal flame!

Throughout young Tut's reign, a council governed the land, running state affairs on his behalf, as they thought he was too young to take control. The leader of that council was known as "Eye"; when interpreted metaphysically, this correctly explains the inner eye that is always watching over us. Also remember that, through the myth, this area is known as the "doorway to 'EA'".

The story goes on to inform us that, after Tutankhamen's death, his wife, Ankhetzunamun, was given in marriage to Eye, who was her supposed grandfather. In other words, she returned back into the responsibility of her higher mind – or her family lineage. This then gave the emotional mind (or right brain), which she represents symbolically, the right to begin again.

Some say that the boy-king reigned for ten years (from the age of nine to the age of nineteen), but this story differs, depending on the land where you hear it told. I have been told, throughout the old countries, that he reigned from the age of twelve to the age of twenty-one years. So we will continue with the first set of numbers, and explain them correctly through the codes of the Sacred Numerology.

We know that the number ten (10) represents "through change, I am exalted up into my next level of intellect". The codes add up again when we understand that Tut supposedly died at the age of nineteen (19), and we see that the numbers (1 + 9 = 10) are carried up into the next Divine equation; and this explains the next level, where we balance our inner knowledge. This Divine equation becomes a mirror of two worlds coming together – the old and new – where they never argue with one another.

The number ten (10) is also an extreme code of responsibility; it is an added value of self, an earning of self. It is the first number of the double digits; therefore, when we think of this number, the unconscious mind opens us up into the next level. We move into the new realm of intellect, where our language changes. The "I Am" becomes the "We Are".

We cannot go back to our old worlds of thought; we must continue to move forward. Through earning the five days of freedom – or the five virgin births – this is known as the fourth day. It is where the hymen shreds from the glands, and the ego has birthed itself to become free. No more restrictions exist. We have delivered ourselves up into the unconscious mind, and we are able to hear and see the world through the understanding of Extra-Terrestrial Communication. Are you seeing the royal approach to life becoming your palace of worthiness? Automatically, honesty reigns supreme, and you speak your truth naturally and purposely.

After the tomb was unearthed and catalogued, we know that a mosquito bit Lord Carnarvon on the upper right cheek, and he died soon after. He had earned the mathematics of his thoughts, and his mind had accrued through his own ploy. In other words, through the Divine equation that his Oracle released to him – which was his penance as to how he had to receive his karmic reward – and also through his own innocence, his death was pronounced. Through the importance of this find in Egypt, he had to receive his highest reward, and that was his penance for being jealous of the importance given to Howard Carter for the job that he had accomplished.

Carter returned to London, satisfied with his work. He died never having received an honour, from either the Egyptian or British governments, for the countless hours of sacrifice that he had committed himself to in discovering the greatest Seal of Humanity.

I will, I salute the gift he gave us.

Your Notes:

CHAPTER THIRTY ONE

Our Intellectual Light

As the years of my wisdom have opened up in me, I now understand that each period of my gestation into the unconscious mind has been part of my own ascension process – that is, each phase has been a step of my climb up the rungs of Jacob's ladder. Throughout my journey, I often wondered why my first trance experience was of Egyptian energy, but now I know; I had to start at the top and work backwards. It is all about reversing, you will remember. We now understand how the fourth dimension comes into our being: it is through the belief of self! This belief anoints us as we gather and bring the dexterity of our intellect together.

When I am focused, I am receiving and transforming what needs to be brought through and transmitted in that moment; this occurs in humans in exactly the same way that it does in a radio. That is fourth-dimensional reality, and it is available to all of us. When I am in focus, with many words coming through, I trust that I can find a point within all those words from which to begin; I trust that, in the midst of all that is coming through to me, an energy or emotion exists that I can accept and understand. And when I find it, that is where I begin. To do that, I tune in through the consciousness, which gives me a variety of stories. I react in the same way as the little black box used for tuning radio aerials. We call this an SWR meter (SWR represents "standing wave ratio", and this is the ratio of the amount of the signal standing in the coaxial cable, to the amount of signal radiating from the antenna). I can tune my own aerial in to many frequencies – and when I am in, I am in. It doesn't matter where you are situated – or which country you live in on this planet – if you contact me for an answer, I can always read you, through your emotions. My purpose is to teach you the truth; whatever information I have is yours to use, once you can believe in you. I have earned the respect from the Divine Consciousness.

Let us talk about the psyche for a moment. The psyche is the vibration that filters through from the unconscious mind. The challenge that you give yourself occurs once you silence your mind, as it then begins to enter into other worlds. It is at this stage that you must always remain focused and balanced. If you are not in your stillness, you remain entangled in your past; and this is where your mind has no direction to home in on, and, as a result, it will tend to run away from you. Mental detachment happens when people are living their reality through the entanglement of their own fear.

Our intellectual light manifests only when the mind is focused. When the ego (or conscious mind) releases, through learning to trust itself, it is then collected into the subconscious (or emotional mind), and the emotional mind automatically trusts the next level, which is the unconscious mind (or Higher Self). You cannot doubt yourself for a moment!

When you first begin to reach up into the heavens, it is a step by step introduction, where your Higher Self begins speaking through you. It is autonomically tuning you in to the right frequencies in order to prepare you for the Collective to come through loud and clear. Your body awakens and releases to let the force fields speak. Thus, your respectful light shines through you having earned your self!

In the same way that an astronaut is plugged into the oxygen from his spacecraft, so, too, are we plugged into the Collective. I am explaining your next positive breath; this is God at work, and God is the light in you. That light is your intelligence, and you create and release your freedom through accepting it. Please remember that your light comes through the power of love, not through the love of power.

It is through your internal growth that your external growth expands. You are seeing and learning the Laws of the Universe, which make up the fourth dimension. The fourth-dimensional mind is where we are simultaneously awake in this world and living in the dream world – it is a state of collectiveness – in other words, we are asleep and awake at the same time. The dream world is the world of invisibility; it is the world of the unconscious mind that is already known to and within us all.

Don't turn your back on yourself through your own ignorance!

We do not repeat the same mistakes once we are able to understand and believe in ourselves. Every human is accepting his own behaviour; he is doing what he has evolved into through the Laws of the Universe. We are all on this journey of discovering our self-worthiness.

The more we align, the more we expand our mentality. This stimulates the nervous system to where it can reinvest in itself. All this becomes the standard we bear; the flag that flies in the wind and echoes throughout our body. That metaphor is called your "hologram". The quieter you are within, the more you hear the real you; it is your own Soul manifesting and purifying itself. Go for it! Trust it! Believe it! Become it!

Your Notes:

CHAPTER THIRTY TWO

The Three Scholars

When I was reading the Bible in its reverse order (i.e., from back to front, as previously explained), I was amazed to understand the wisdom that the stories foretold. I began to realize that I was reading about my own journey and the expectations that I was asked to surrender to. I ask that you not judge me; rather, just listen to the interpretation through my understanding. If you could accept and understand that you have the opportunity to reveal, through your own enquiring mind, the hidden codes embedded within the stories in the Bible, you would realize that we all share this same story – there is only one story, remember, and it is the story of the Collective. Once you recognized that truth, you would see into, not look at, this language of telepathic communication that I am explaining to you, and then you would realize that it is the next step up into humanity's earnings. If we each lived our responsibilities as we touch and hear our own feelings and thoughts, this world would be a better place for us all.

Back to my own interpretations and understanding. First, I had to understand the story of Mary and the virgin birth of Jesus. This story is identical to that of Isis and the virgin birth of her son, Horus. Mithras, who supposedly lived many years before Horus, was also the son of a virgin birth. Through the codes, this name is "Myt-he-rha-us", which means "through the myth of my heavenly energy, I release into the heavenly ascension through understanding my Soul". That's nice, isn't it? You will find that this story repeats itself over and over again in the Bible (as well as throughout the myths of many cultures), and it has to repeat itself, as this repetition is how the story embeds into our genetic inheritance. This is the light that becomes God.

The last time I journeyed back to Egypt, I wanted to study the Arabic language, as I was much more confident with my knowledge of understanding the codes of the temples. I wanted to hear how they spoke and pronounced their words in Arabic. I explained that, in Arabic, Joseph is "Youseph", and it represents "your self"! Joseph is the ego – our left brain and conscious world. Mary is "Mha-Rha-EA", which, when interpreted through the codes, means "mastering the Rah of God". Mary is the emotional mind – our right brain and subconscious world, which tune us up into the unconscious mind.

I would like to thank my amazing Egyptian teachers for showing me the correct pronunciation of their alphabet, as well as for explaining the missing codes that I had so long searched for. I had to return to where it all began in order to discover my self; and, as always, the more I go back into the past and understand it, the more the future is placed before me. I began to realize, as I read the myths and brought them together through understanding the language of Metaphysics, that everything that I had been taught over the years was exactly right.

One afternoon in Luxor, I met with three scholars, one each from Egypt, Somalia, and the Sudan. Their names fascinated me: Abraham, Isaac, and Jacob. In the beginning, the language between them and me was hesitant, as we learned to read each other's energy. We all had an enquiring mind about what each of us expected of the other. But, which one of us would begin first? They understood who I was and what I represented, and their respect melted my heart. Once the dust had settled around us, we spent many happy hours in each other's company.

The three of them could understand one another, yet each spoke in his own native way. One of them pronounced the name of Jesus as "Ye-Shwa"; another, as "Ye-zues"; and the third, as "He-zeus". Now, hang on a minute, what was that about Zeus? Wasn't he the principal deity of Greece – or, as the Egyptians explained to me, "God of all things"? Through the codes, He is very important, as it interprets as, "heavenly energy". Was this symbol that we know as Jesus, in reality, an interpretation of the heavenly energy of Zeus? When we relate that story to ourselves, we see that Jesus Christ is a metaphor for the evolution of each human – the heavenly energy of our inner light!

The four of us talked on into the afternoon and evening, and it was one of the most enlightening days I had spent in many years. I received the answers to questions I had been given twenty six years before, which had now been confirmed for me in the physical sense. I was back on the earth, and I learned that everything I had been taught through the esoteric worlds all those years previous was true and correct. I was elated, as I had carried this wisdom on my shoulders for many years, before my confidence gave me the go-ahead to use it. I had to wait until I had been delivered into the wisdom of Egypt in order to feel free to release it.

We spent the next day with me talking, and them listening, to the story about what I had received. Their faces ached from smiling so much. More importantly, I heard and accepted their stories, watching as they filtered through into me.

I now understood that the stories of Jesus and Zeus, together, symbolically represent your left brain, whereas Christ represents your right brain. When he became Jesus Christ, his reflection – or light – began through the nourishment that he had released through his own Divinity, just as he had released his twelve Apostles – or strands of DNA – all through his understanding and acceptance of self.

Your Notes:

CHAPTER THIRTY THREE

The First Four Books Of The New Testament

The first four books of the New Testament (which we also refer to as the Gospels) are the stories of Matthew, Mark, Luke, and John. It took me a few years to unravel and decode the names of these four important books, as I had to be in the right frame of mind to accept the evolution of all languages. In other words, I had to release and hear the right sounds at the time of my reading the Bible so that I could accept the codes through the answers that I received.

Matthew, in the German language, is pronounced "Matthaus". Through the codes, it means "MA-AT-house" – or, more precisely, "the house of Ma'at". In Arabic, it is pronounced nearly the same: "Ma'at-hous". In English, of course, it is Matthew – or "Maat-hew". The word hue means "tint or colour", so, once again, we are reminded of the rainbow we arc as our intellect releases itself. I remember as a child, on the rare occasions when it rained in the Outback, my father would stand outside and shout to the heavens, "Send her down, Huey!"

Mark is pronounced "Merke-beh", in Arabic, with an emphasis on the last syllable. The word "merkebeh" means "boat without a sail". Through the Sacred Alphabet, it is "Merke-bja"; thus, symbolically, it is informing us of the "Mark of the Beast"! Now, hold on; we will try this again! If the regent number is 666, what is this paragraph beginning to tell us? These coded numbers speak of our opportunity to gather and master our own mind. Does it also explain to us that we each are the boat gliding through the Universal Consciousness by means of the strength that we find within our own belief? The symbol on the flag of the Isle of Corfu in Greece has a small boat without a rudder – with such a boat, it is up to you as to how you sail and in what direction you set your course. In other words, you are responsible for steering your own vessel and navigating your own journey! I will remind you again of the four boats that were discovered at each of the four corners of the Great Pyramid in Egypt.

Luke has been recorded as the youngest healer – or doctor – on the planet. Luke is pronounced "Feluka", in Arabic; and a feluka, which has its own sail, is a larger boat than the merkebeh. The wind is the healer; it is the Breath of God that automatically lifts us up into the angelic realms.

In Arabic, the name John is pronounced "Youh Haarness", which represents how you support yourself in order to receive your Spiritual strength. "Youh Haarness" also means "Your Highness". In the German language, John is Johannes. When interpreted through the codes, John means "you and the light within".

So let us now bring those four books together, and I will explain a story to you. You are here to sail through the seven seas. Through your house of Ma'at, you will sail in your Mark in all directions, as you do not have a rudder to steer your boat. Your boat is your body, and, when your boat has no rudder, you have no control. You must earn that rudder in order to be able to steer yourself towards the direction that you wish to move into – this is the tempering of the mind.

So we enter into the Book of Luke, where we begin to become more aware of the self. Through hearing our thoughts, we connect with the ethereal energy of the Collective of all, and then, through the wind – or the Breath of God – we set sail in the direction of the next positive thought.

The Book of John is the light that we have found within; through this light, we ascend up Into the unconscious mind, where we earn the royal name of "Your Highness". Those four books also explain the four directions to us – our north, south, east, and west. Through the laws of Shamanism, the four directions explain how we can direct ourselves to receive the connection to our inner healing station – or Medicine Wheel.

Again, remember that the Bible was written in a hidden language – or codes – which evolved through the way those High Priests had been trained in the seminaries of the past. The language of Metaphysics challenged them to reach up and beyond; in the same way as this language has become a challenge for you as you strive to accept your inner self.

Neither the language, nor the journey was ever intended for the person who is still learning through others! Every human has to reach a peak of his own perfection in order to be exalted. Through the merge of Christianity, which has been brought through for us all to placate, is the next step for us to conciliate, through the advancement of understanding what had previously been written.

Jesus gathered his twelve Disciples – which are also the twelve Disciplines of the Eastern traditions and the twelve metals of Alchemy that create our tone (or the music we create when we speak). Those twelve Disciplines vibrate down through our twelve internal organs, where, in order for our DNA to release, the twelve strands must complete, not compete! In short, if we go back into every language, we will hear the stories of the twelve!

Throughout the Old Testament, the story explains to us that there are twelve emotional tribes of people on the planet, and they differentiate from one another through the way that they think, act, and become. Those twelve tribes have earned their own tribal laws, and they have collected their own emotions and consequentially, their fears. Believe it or not, the fears each tribe collects creates the variety of diseases known only to that tribe!

Throughout the beginning of the Bible, only twelve tribes are explained, as this is continuing the moment from our evolution. All this intelligence has become our history, and, until the evolution of mankind expands itself, no extension of the tribes can occur. In other words, until humans realize their own potential, these numbers will remain the same.

Once we have learned to unfold ourselves up into the next level, we will find that those old tribal heritages will all tune in to becoming one evolution. Now that so many of us have begun to search deeper within ourselves for an alternative pathway, perhaps those twelve tribes will have the opportunity to release the stricture of their own confinement. All tribes must become equal in order for us to change the status quo.

Here is an example from my own life of same tribe. Many

years ago, I was working in Sydney as a Consultant. One morning, I had a feeling that it was going to be a powerful day; I knew that I was about to learn something new. As I was about to go to my desk to begin my work, I received a phone call from my friend, Julie, who had recently moved south to Melbourne, hoping to live in a cooler climate.

We talked through her difficulties, and then she explained to me that it was very hot there, and she was wearing her old blue and white top with white shorts – she had nearly thrown these out, owing to her move south. When we lived up north together, she'd practically lived in that outfit. As she said those words, a woman walked into the room; she wore a pair of white capri and a blue and white striped top. I received a message that the same woman would come to me for a reading later that day.

My first client arrived, so I cut the conversation short and said good-bye to Julie. A woman came to my desk wearing a white top and a pair of blue and white striped slacks. When she told me that her name was Julie, I was not surprised. During the course of that day, six women named Julie came to me for consultation, and they all dressed in exactly the same colours of blue and white.

The emotional difficulties that those six Julies had were exactly the same emotions that were troubling my friend Julie in Melbourne; three of them were born in the same month, and the other three cusped at either end of that month. Six Julies all born within thirty-three days of one another, all dressed the same, and all having exactly the same problems at the same time. I was being initiated into another connection that related to the twelve tribes, where each tribe of our personalities creates the same experience for them to realign themselves with; they are given the same names, are born around the same time, and so forth. All these experiences are connected through the emotional intellect we speak.

Our intelligence clones itself through the unconscious mind, and, as we grow up into our own inheritance, we conduit with others of same mind who have the same emotional difficulties and values of self. Those difficulties set a pattern, and, through our fear claiming its sole right, we trap our emotions within. As individuals, our twelve channels become as one, and then those twelve channels become our mind; this is where we clone ourselves unconsciously out into our own reflection. Upon releasing our inner truth, we form a relationship with others who think as we think. I have just explained to you how we begin to understand the opening of our twelve strands of our DNA!

Treat your thoughts and mind with the greatest respect. Do not look back on it; but, instead, please learn to look into it. Maybe now we can begin to understand the story of the first Pharaoh of Egypt and why he held himself under his own command. As the next generation of each Pharaoh continued through his own lineage, he learned to accept the other premises that each forthcoming generation could inherit. Until we came to Akhenaton!

Your Notes:

CHAPTER THIRTY FOUR

Unfolding The Myth

Throughout the many years of my journey, I have had the pleasure of unfolding the myth as to how our intelligence inherits itself. It is equivalent to the body's alpha waves, where my twelve tribes have released their restrictions; they are now working for me on an outer level, living quite happily in my own force field. That is the myth explaining itself back to me. It happens to me physically, as I now live in the realms of my unconscious mind, and so I have a miracle in every moment. Through releasing my information into this book, another myth has opened up and presented itself to me.

I have now symbolically birthed the four heads of Hathor through my auric layers, where my mind is free. Those heads have repeated themselves on another layer, and again on the next layer, and so on. This is relevant to the symbol of Guan Ean (or Quanyin), the Bodhisattva, which represents the Asian philosophies. Through the Metaphysical language of the Asian understanding, my body has become the Bodhisattva energy, which is the collected strength and power of the emotional mind. I can now hear and equate my mind as I speak to others. Once again, my hologram is announcing to me new possibilities as to the extension of the human evolution – and so my life continues.

As I walk my teachings in many lands, I see the reflections of people that I have met before in my own country. I don't run up to them anymore to try to communicate with them – they don't understand me; they speak a different language. I have now grown up, faced my wisdom, and become my own reflection. The tribe that you belong to is echoed right around this wonderful planet – that is what keeps the Collective connected – we are all one.

You need to walk through your darkness (what has already been) in order to understand and accept your intellectual light. A greater field of strength is for you to become your darkness and thank your fear, so that you will earn the right to your light (what will become). We all have to find our inner strength in order to face the darkness within us – in order to free our mind. As we search ourselves microscopically on an inner level, we see how God reflects it back to us on an outer level – that is, from a wider perspective.

Did you know that the dark matter of the Universe is still a challenge to many scientists, yet it all is one and the same, all of which is mirroring itself?

Ascension is the process of working on your intelligence and believing in yourself. Step outside yourself to rescue your mind from time to time, and remember the words of the Lord Buddha: "Pause and breathe deeply, to create time to smell the flowers". Allow your life force to filter through every cell in your body, to ease you into your everlasting life.

Through the Laws of the Universe, there is no right or wrong – it is an autonomic reaction to our thoughts permanently balancing the creation of consciousness. We who understand and believe in the Universal Laws, are just a step above yesterday. We searched for something greater, as something still needed to be satisfied within us. Discovering something new at each search point, we studied it, and then we moved on. We searched beyond the third dimension, and into the fourth, seeking the next challenge: creating a better understanding of how we can first enhance ourselves and then advance the world. As I look out there are a few heads that are equal to mine, as I shift my eyes lower there are many who are right beneath me and as I look down there is a large mist that protects those who still have the journey ahead to face themselves.

You are your own time machine, wrapped in layers of veils that are the inheritance of your innocence and fear. Remove your veils, one at a time; this will give you the opportunity to go back into your past and remain there, or to learn from your inheritance – and then your journey can continue and you can earn the freedom to create your future. Become your own teacher, it has always been available to you. Maybe now you are ready to hear your God within. The choice is yours. Remember the Lid of Palenque, seated at the controls of his own spaceship, carved with the capabilities of how we can extend the human thought. Go forth and multiply your thoughts.

Your Notes:

CHAPTER THIRTY FIVE

The Responsibility Of Accepting Our Consequences

As I peruse the words in my books, I periodically experience moments of indecision as to how I have explained some of the information. This story has taken more than twenty years of my life to bring together in its correct assumption, and so, of course, I would like to express it in its correctness – that is, in a way that was as true to the way that it had been delivered unto me by the Universe.

One of the biggest shocks to my many students over the years – from the carpet weaver in the mountains of Turkey to the business executive in New York – was the information regarding pregnancy. The reaction was always the same. I watched as the words I spoke sank in, and each one turned to the other – first for support and then in amazement, as they found the courage to relate and share their many personal stories.

I had touched their hearts, and this precious time that they shared with one another gave them the opportunity to remember their own thoughts at the time when they first realized they were pregnant. I asked them to remove the masks that they had hidden behind, in their innocence, so many years before. They had earned their wisdom when they could look back through their own history of thought. Of course, we think we need the next generation to come through in order to keep the planet alive; that is our progress being postulated. It also gives our excuses an abeyance, which we think gives us the right to stall time. We all have to learn to grow up! There are many stages of personal growth, and we all walk through the same doorway to enter into the Hall of Records. Enjoy your journey of discovering the self! Look after those precious children that you have brought into your laws. Teach them well. Guide them through your love; for, that is how they each will learn to become their own self – and a citizen of the planet to become the glyph of light that reflects throughout the Universe.

I remember a few years ago when I conducted a seminar in Japan, where a woman asked me what would happen to the world if there were no additive for the next generation. "What would happen to us all if there were no continuation of our family ties?" she said. So we used her country as an example, and I explained that just twenty-five years ago we were warned globally of an epidemic of overpopulation! It had been forecast that, the way we were heading, the world would triple its population in the next fifty years. To put this another way, what had taken us thousands of years to produce could triple in forty-plus years!

What does this story explain to us? The figures in Japan at the time of that seminar were 1.7 children to each family. So, as they reached maturity and throughout their working life, those 1.7 children – times the total number of families in that country – would be the adults responsible for millions of the elderly populace. We are talking here in regard to releasing Karma; that is, the results of our actions are placed on young shoulders. You see, up to now, only a few of us have wanted to take on the responsibility of accepting our own consequences.

That young woman had one child, and so I asked her what she could foresee happening in her land. "Something I have always wished for is no high-rise apartments. My dream is for my grandchild to be able to see more of the earth and sky than I have been able to," was her answer. I had never thought of the world that way! I asked her why she only had one child, and she replied, "We both have had to work, and, besides, we have no room to place another bed in our already crowded apartment. We would love to have the opportunity to buy a car, but it will take years until we have earned that reward." Goodness! I had never thought of that, either.

Many countries have this same problem. China was an even greater experience for me to learn from. For over four hundred years, their laws have held a one-child policy for those who live in the cities, and no more than two, under special circumstances, for those who live in the outer provinces.

The latest information, from those who are responsible for the figures on the growth of the world population, is that governments are now telling people to have more children in order to keep up a balance of humanity. Balance for whom? Onto which part of society are we placing the responsibility? Is this all for the next generation to inherit? Twenty-five years ago, our governments told us to do exactly the opposite of what they are telling us now!

If this directive could shift to its opposite in twenty-five years' time, our governments have a lot to answer for – and, more importantly, a lot to accept as to the consequences of what their predecessors deemed through their wisdom (or lack thereof) for the good of all! Our education has opened up our intelligence, and we have climbed up the ladder of our own success. We have accepted our own responsibilities; we have grown up, and now we require a more peaceful attitude to enhance our mind. We have become more adult in our thinking, and our wisdom is claiming its own existence. Just look at what we have accomplished in all fields – technology, medical sciences, etc. – over the last hundred years. Where is the detriment to all that? We have come such a long way.

Women are having their children much later in life now, as they are free to have their own career first. Governments and companies have given them the comforts of childcare throughout their working hours, and this collaboration is becoming a global consensus. Women also have a choice now in regard to how many children they wish to have; gone are the days when Grandmother was available to rear the young – she is proudly out there working on her own career!

We are releasing the expectations of the previous generation, and, through the expansion of our own wisdom, our mind is becoming freer. The pressure is subsiding, and so the Collective Consciousness will add up our mathematics on our behalf – and, more importantly, it will do so without our interference – in order to relate to us how we can make this world a better place for all. However, we still have a few important things for us to tidy up first.

CHAPTER THIRTY SIX

Your Journey Now

I can go on and on extolling the results of our thinking – or which dis-ease we will create for our future inheritance – when we are tied up with ignoring our thoughts and not earning the results of our own actions. We can heal anything when we believe in ourselves; we even have our own stem cell research station embedded in the pituitary gland. We have not made a mistake; we have gained a momentous learning through earning the experiences that the Universe has delivered to us. We have earned the right to know when enough is enough; this is where we place our priority back into ourselves.

We earn the levels of self-love through our innocence unfolding – through believing in ourselves. Slowly, we walk the hills and valleys of the land and seem to have a need to keep on birthing our families, as we think that they are the experiences of adjustment that will help the earth to mother itself. We then have the possibility to feel through this love, and, as we open up our hearts, we are able to return this gift of love to help others.

Genesis 3:16 explains how the cells of the body dance to their own tune in order to create a repetition of self. Those are the teachings of the Laws of the Universe, which we also refer to as God. We are all one! God is Love! Let us get this Religion of Science right so that we can release the Science of Religion, which is the quality of the light we find within. We have never made mistakes; we have gained millions of experiences, all of which have advanced us through releasing the wisdom that is inside us all.

Understand the myths that have been verbally handed down through time. They are an inner language that explains how we, as humanity, have believed in ourselves; how we have learned to think so that our next thought can return and deliver the next positive moment.

From time to time, when going back into my memory bank to recall a story, I would make a mistake with the spelling of a word. My wonderful, friendly computer would display the word for me with an explanation to the next word I was to write. Metaphysics is also the language of the computer, and its codes have created themselves through the Laws of the Universe, using the numbers one (1) and zero (0). These digits release through the codes as, "I am my Soul". The language – or code – of the computer is stored as:

100111011100010101100001010111100.

Try to decipher the sentences from that code. (Please refer to book my book "Decoding the Sacred Alphabet and Numerology".)

Hopefully, I have taken you on a journey of self-discovery – a journey that I have personally stepped through in order to release the medicine woman (Shaman) within me and announce you into the mathematical codes of your consciousness. I have written these stories to explain your freedom to you; this is the way for the journey of your next thought to allow both you and humanity to prosper.

Throughout my books, I have introduced you into the codes of the Laws of the Universe – which we also call God, this **G**reatest **O**racle of the **D**ivine, which is also the Oracle of Life – in order to reintroduce you to your thoughts. Remember that every thought you think is the most important moment in your life; also, it releases throughout the Collective Consciousness and refracts the history of mankind.

After that, came my explanation of the reasoning behind sexuality, and why it is so important in regard to how you honour the intellect of your ego. Connected to that is the importance of your thoughts as to the dis-eases that you are creating for yourself by hanging onto your past experiences. They are each a blessing that we inherit in order to find the strength to explain to our ego the importance of itself! I next explained how to understand the codes of how and why people die. We then journeyed together up into the Cosmic Law of the Ocean, and I explained its importance to our Soul. We have looked at the sacredness of the Alphabet and Numerology in order to understand how we have inherited and accepted our intellect. We have journeyed into the understanding of myths and how they have embedded themselves in and throughout the biblical hierarchy. Together, we learned how the energy moves through our home and workplace. Finally, we ascended into the Collective Law of Extra-Terrestrial Intelligence.

We must remember that our body is 90 per cent water; this is the highest receptor of all, and it is what keeps us alive. Can you begin to see how important you are to every other human?

Every time we think a thought, we are automatically challenging the molecular structure of our home base. It is a simple task to take your thoughts into your own mind, to allow them to rest in peace. That is what we call a "meditation", which allows our heart to open, freeing the light of intelligence through stimulating every cell in our body. Allow your choices of thought to be free and not become restricted through other people's expectations. Remember that the body language is a continuing repertoire that is hidden from you – and yet, it is right there in front of you every time you look ahead. It is "right in front of your nose", so to speak. See everything around you – all of it is waiting for you, designed by God to attract your attention and to answer your questions. This is the glory of the unconscious mind working on your behalf! These are the laws of the Sages – or the "Soul's ages".

Do you recall the information regarding the "bat" and the "butterfly", which are situated up in the pituitary area of the brain? The sphenoid bone ("bat") supports the gland that rocks and rolls, weighing our thinking in regard to the thought that tips into either the left or the right hemisphere; and this explains the repetitious mistakes we create. This area is where we first begin to stimulate the feelings that reign over us. Remember that we see the "butterfly" when we look up to the inner heavenly realms; these wonderful species permanently migrate all around the planet searching for their seasons. Their senses are produced through their feelers – or antennae – in order to carry them forward to accomplish their own result! We humans do the same. We release our antennae through own intellectual light's stimulation of our feelings, which tunes us into our unconscious mind. The "bat", which helps us produce our sonic sound, can only be delivered to us when we have opened our heart to ourselves; and this is where we view ourselves – and the self – from these heavenly kingdoms and back down into our earthly realms. In other words, the Universe – or God – is delivering us all the same migratory path to consecrate our own transformation. Please enjoy your journey at every step.

Once again, Revelations expresses it best: "And there appeared a great wonder in Heaven, a woman clothed with the Sun and the Moon under her feet, and upon her head a crown of twelve stars." (Revelations 12:1.)

Your Notes:

CHAPTER THIRTY SEVEN

ET Cells, Spaceships, Glyphs Of Light In The Sky, Star Seed and Indigo Children

I enjoyed revising this book drawing from the earnings of the last four years of my education. There is a difference between learning and earning. Learning comes from explanations that you receive from someone else. Earnings are released to you from your inner self. I would like to share my current knowledge into Extra-Terrestrial Intelligence (ETI), where I have acquired additional insights regarding the Extra-Terrestrial (ET) cells that are implanted in humanity during our gestation, once the brain has completed its formation.

In the past four years, I have been repeatedly astounded that we are implanted through our gestation with each layer of cells (cellular layers) that are mathematically cohabiting with and through one another to collect an inner language. This language of awareness serves as a foundation for us to continue on to revere (to feel deep respect for, whether we are here on the earth or have moved on to our next educational step on the other side) our future generations.

The download process (on a cellular level) occurs when the ET cells are introduced into the gestation of humanity mathematically. No, I am not too sure on all of my verifications right now, as my mind is receiving information in steps and stairs where it has become a very slow-moving continuous walk towards bringing the mathematics, balancing with the science (the sci-essence) of the information together. As this is the year where we are revising the nine separate books of "Decoding the Mind of God", each with added information.

Allow me to explain on my current understanding. The first cluster of cells, the largest cells in the body to be implanted in the body of females, are situated high between the upper inner thighs, which is connected so some say to the ovaries. Through my education and understanding, this area of our body is referred to as the lungs of consciousness, with these cells intricately threaded through our reproductive organs up to the navel region. Once these cells have calibrated mathematically amongst themselves, the information is then free to converse with the rest of the body. Now, do you understand how we are implanted mathematically during our gestation, forming the cellular structure before birth?

This has been correlated to and with the mathematics of our DNA, which coordinates the synchronisation with the rest of the body when we have reached a peak or turning point in our performance (emotional intelligence), through us being in our moment of progressive thought!

Once we have birthed, the newborn child must adjust to its new universe through the energies released in the home. This home becomes its initial universe. The child sensitivity absorbs the energy released by the rest of the family, which can sometimes unsettle the child. However, once it feels the nurturing love vibrations are reciprocated, the little one can then relax and their life continues on.

Please remember that the emotion of love overpowers all. Love, as an emotion, changes and refurbishes our DNA as we open up the next step of our intellect through the vibrational changes of the Soul's energy. The emotion of love is released through the rearranging (reconfiguration) of our heartbeat through the feelings that we have released towards this little one who has entered our family linage. The little one feels this expression through our release, and this loving feeling has autonomically (self-governed) been altered through the vibrations of our heart, where they completely harmonize and rebalance. Love vibrates into a language of feelings that all the family accept through the heart and can use to explain their own vocabulary. Through the mathematical adjustment of time, as we step forward, this releases its message through to our brain.

As we continue on with our lives, we are educated, go to work, find a partner, and the family begins to grow, we may find ourselves overwhelmed, wondering where we went wrong. Someone may suggest meditation as a means to quiet the mind. The past three years, marked by COVID shocking us to the core, losing our loved ones, and the exorbitant living costs, we are realizing that the whole planet has been pushed beyond its normality, emotionally. Our plans have been altered, our thinking has gone awry, and we have had to rearrange our thinking to suit each new moment of our expenditure (circumstances). The current statistics demonstrate that millions have succumbed to the pandemic globally, with numbers still growing daily. This contagious pandemic has earned quite a large footprint to carry itself forward, compelling us to learn to come "home" to ourselves and yearn to learn to earn our futuristic knowledge.

I am trying to explain to you the make-up of the inner self, known to us, as we start to collect out new found intelligence, as the Higher Self. It is the vibration that we learn to adhere with through the compatibility with our Soul and facilitating the release and harmonization of our inner turmoil, intricately connected to the lymphatic system.

I explain this to my new students that this most important system is, metaphorically speaking, the "Umbrella of God". This system is threaded throughout the whole body and is recognised in many cultures as God's protective canopy. I have now been asked to refer to it as the "**G**reatest **O**racle of the **D**ivine." It sits within and lovingly waits for us to fall and is always there to resurrect and protect us.

Through years of research decoding the ancient texts such as the Egyptian Book of the Dead, Egyptian Philosophies, Mayan Principles, Biblical text, Indian and Asiatic Influences, I have earned the knowledge of the Universal Language, explaining the wisdom passed down by those who walked before us. They were remarkably astute in their time, where everything became a conundrum, legend, or mystery that we had to abide by, prompting us to elevate our thinking in order to release the next step of our inner truth and for us to advance from our previous education (understanding).

In reference to the large cells, they can only open up once we have ended our old life (advanced our thinking) and the new existence of our intelligence begins, whether it be through a woman falling pregnant through her sacrificing herself to others, where she brings through the next generation to take up her challenges, or we have come to the end of our tether where we begin thinking it is time to start our life all over again!

This next shift is delivered unto (from above) us in a much higher degree, in a totally new format. We refer to it as discovering our inner journey, where we are reading from our inner "Library of Books", or Bible. Additionally, I will repeat the Germanic term for their DNS which is our DNA, as "Bibliothek," representing the technical knowledge of our inner sacredness, which through our own DNA is known as our spiritual (inner) journey. As we accept this effort of validation, the heart then begins on restructuring our dichotomy - these are our irreconcilable differences. Through the heart recalibrating with the brain, they both begin to vibrate, working together to harmonize and balance our wholeness. This, once again, changes the autonomy (self-governing) of our heart beat, which alerts the cells to open new passages of information. These changes and rearrangements of our thought processes and word structure set our body to fire up to release our new inner dictionary.

Through accepting this new information, we start a journey of self-discovery. On reflection of the old myths and legends foretold that we gain a profound understanding of metaphysics. This aligns with our comprehension of Shamanic Vibrations, as well as various cultural and philosophical systems, including the Biblical, Egyptian, Mayan, Tibetan, Indian, Arabic, and Asian Philosophies, among many others. They are all explaining the same identical story in their language; essentially convey the same story. As the self becomes centered through the power of love and respect, we release new information from our inner self with a permanent smile. I did this all by myself! With our newfound confidence, we have a strong urge to continue on.

As our faith and belief in Self begins to awaken, these large cells commence emitting new signals to one another. Through this exchange of information, they become aware of new feelings emerging from our heart, flushing away the past throughout our body. There is a consciousness within these cells that their time is approaching. These large cells start paying attention to the conversations inferred on an inner level, as there are progressive changes developing through each person's vocabulary. In this process, we ascend our inner ladder (also referred to as Jacobs Ladder), of this long forgotten or previously buried intelligence. In the meantime, these large cells have absorbed every thought and experience in your life to this moment. Take your time! Can you imagine how much information is passed on and re-threaded through to the largest cells as our intelligence unfolds throughout our life? We are quite a magnificent time machine, aren't we?

The development of this intelligence unfolding is: the process of how we think each thought begins to release from the cells. The smallest cells release their information onto the next cells, and they in turn exhaust their information. Then each layer that has forfeited its mathematical intellect (information), diminish and so they say, die. Supposedly, newly updated cells are then released to take their place to re-thread and connect with the internal dictionary of our tribal heritage (family) or our own individual DNA.

New information is then released. This continues on throughout the life you are living in your cellular memory, until you have earned the intellectual time for the largest cells to step in. Now remember, they are the first cells to be implanted and the last cells to awaken, as they are the largest cells that have the ability to become a store house for our inner knowledge, for us to be able to release the wisdom appropriately through our thoughts processing each other, at the right moment.

This entire process unfolds in concordance with the right hemisphere of your brain, as it steps forward and opens you up to the emotional factors (aspects) of Self by adjusting the mathematical frequencies of your inner knowledge. As a collective, this advancement leads to the attainment of an autonomic (self-governed) declared state of freedom throughout your mind. The next major advancement is the opening of your heart, where it re-fibrillates itself with new informational fibres, received from and through these large cells. Through this advanced change, this allows the heart to rewire its own information and convey new or advanced messages (revised emotional factors), to reprogram the brain. In cohabitating (embracing) these new ideas, your wisdom enters into new dimensions of time, which adds to your inner dictionary. This advances our self-respect more eloquently. In the context of Egyptology and the Book of the Dead, I am explaining the analogy of weighing the feather against the heart, where the ego, symbolized by the crocodile and other raucous beasts attempt to hold you back. Your ego still thinks it has a priority right to control you.

As our wisdom is released, these large cells are free to cohabitate with other like-minded cells, ascending through our DNA towards the heart. The heart then creates a new conversation as your emotional feelings experience an upward swing through a more substantial compatibility being released. This automatically advances the neural pathways in and throughout the right hemisphere of our brain. The left hemisphere is subsequently restructured to align with the concordance (the inner Bible) in terms of how it rearranges its futuristic conversations. Then they both begin to work in unison, revising and enhancing your knowledge comprehensively. Through this process, we open up (unlock) new pockets of information that have been previously endowed in these large cells, through you advancing upon each positive step you take. Can you now begin to understand and appreciate how our DNA is enhanced through this endeavour as we take greater control through the changes and respect we have of our recently released belief in self.

This intelligence then begins to reshape the investiture of your DNA, as you mature into what you have set out to become, which in the future is all through you having superseded your previous intellectual state. As the woman is also the carrier of these large cells, if she doubts her inner knowledge, she forfeits her investiture through her becoming pregnant. This honour she had earned, is then passed on to the DNA of the next generation. Could this honour be the Indigo Children as they have inherited not only their mother's shortcomings, they have also inherited from the previous generations who had the same difficulties in processing their own inner thoughts as well. Remember, this Spiritual journey is one of you looking into yourself, where you discover the innate power and strength within yourself, through the mirrors that the Laws of the Universe or how your Soul returns your gifts back to you.

We owe a great debt of gratitude to Robert Hook for his unwavering dedication in the early 1600s. He tirelessly pursued his research, unravelling the mysteries of the cell and its remarkable capabilities. His tireless efforts spanned many years, providing us with profound insights into our cellular inheritance. Of course, there were many other brilliant minds who contributed to the advancement of our knowledge.

***

Allow me to move on from this subject, and explain the glyphs of light in the sky. During the last four strenuous years, I have been introduced to and shown my next phase of this amazing connection we have with Extra-Terrestrial Intelligence (ETI) that unfolds when we commit to our next step of human evolution. My aim is to explain the reasoning for these awakenings of our mind, enabling you to understand how these events occur and more to the point, why!

I would like to start by sharing the accounts of commercial pilots from various parts of the world. These pilots, responsible for flying us all across the planet, all explain the same conversation about encounters with a spaceship that approached near their plane's cockpit during the dead of the night or throughout the day. They described the movements that the spaceship conveyed to them. All reported their experiences to the appropriate authorities and government agencies of the time, only to be met with a wall of silence and instructions to keep quiet on the subject. I reassured them to take away their fear, assuring them that no harm would befall them. At that time, I shared my own journey, the best way I knew how. Now, I can explain the "how," "when," "where," and, most importantly, the "why" of these encounters.

The sightings do not happen during take-off or landing when the pilot is focused and occupied with the controls. Rather, they transpire during those quiet times when everything is running smoothly. The pilot's mind is at ease and free to allow them to relax into a meditative experience (a quietening of their own mind) where they can start to gather their own thoughts of events and happenings in their own life, or maybe having a quiet conversation with the other pilot and staff in their small cabin, where their minds meet in agreeance to the subject at hand.

During my extensive research and reading many stories of previous legends of Extra-Terrestrial Intelligence (ETI), my thoughts were brought to attention of why it is still the same. Many of these people went on to create and discover brilliance which is still saluting us today. A compelling pattern emerged from my findings and explained to me that the reason the pilot's newfound awareness of the ship appearing outside the cockpit window was created through the positive multiplication of their own thinking. This process was intricately linked to their inner dialogues and the personification and exemplification of their individual thoughts within the sphere of their balanced minds. The ship is a mirror image of the pilot's mind advancing itself through their own belief that this is a continuing thought which through their own faith and belief in Self, can become endowed. (In other words, the ship is a mirror of the pilot's evolving consciousness through their own faith and belief in Self).

Our mind has to become harmonized and balanced on both an inner and outer level, where they become one. If you are balanced in both mind and body, where the endowment you received was collecting, you will begin to realize that it reshaped your gravity fields as to how you were creating and advancing the collective mind within you!

To continue on: a tremendous number of Air Force pilots, from many lands as well as my own, shared the same story as the commercial long distance, pilots. These young men, with a focused mind, were on a mission of representing their country to bring an abeyance of peace to the earth.

Let us not forget the Navy, where many have reported witnessing the space ships emerging from the ocean or soaring through a lonely night sky while on duty on the bridge, or taking a respite thinking over their thoughts before retiring to bed whilst on the deck.

Also, members of the Army had many a story to tell while sacrificing themselves in war-torn countries, through their endeavours to bring a sentience of peace to themselves and to that land. This is a natural phenomenon from our codes of consciousness, being gifted back to us through the collective of the consciousness or, the **G**reatest **O**racle of the **D**ivine.

Here in Australia, I have had many thousands of individuals seeking answers. They have shared their experience of encounters while driving at night on long lonely roads, through the stillness of the outback, which we referred to this awakening as the Min-Min lights, explaining the gas that leaked out of the earth, seen only at night; also, many who walked at night along an empty road. The jackaroo who is alone on large properties, or stations, repairing the fences in the outback with his dog and two horses, one pack horse for the camp and one for himself to ride, for weeks at a time, who always had the ETI to keep him company, where he could think to them and they would give him the answers and more importantly, many of them heard them. The messages imparted by ETI have changed his life! And the stories continue, with thousands of people seeking mental clarity being awakened from their sleep, often by encounters with the enigmatic greys. These experiences have helped them find resolution for the dilemmas that accompanied them to bed.

Do you remember that magnificent movie that deserves a perfect 10, featuring Will Smith - "The Legend of Bagger Vance," where he imparts his wisdom on the golf course? This modern parable is explaining how one's inner and outer worlds have become completely harmonized with one another.

***

These last paragraphs are for me to explain the term "Star Seed", which has gained popularity in today's vernacular. Through the information I have earned through thirty years of education, I thank the universe from keeping me detached from society. My journey was guided solely by the mathematics of the supreme consciousness. In the initial stage, I stumbled, and then began walking towards understanding the inner workings of what is known as the "God Particle".

This is explaining how our inner light is refracted (which is deflected) or retracted (withdrawn) until more information is added to the value of its consistency, through the laws of the supreme consciousness. These laws occasionally provided subtle hints into the convergence of my findings now and then, to assist me to equalize and balance my own mind when it required correction or a change in direction (change of thinking). Yes, I have heard what many others have had to say, as each client comes for verification as to what information they have been given regarding their own journey of self-discovery.
Then, follow me and let us begin.

"Lost in Space," "Star Trek," and then "Star Wars" were huge winners on TV, captivating the younger generation from the late '70s through to the early '90s. "Star Wars" continues to be a lasting source of education where George Lucas explains his version of our inner journey to millions of minds. George Lucas and I had the same mentor, through the most intellectual awareness of Joseph Campbell, who challenged me with the "masks we wear". I was quickly introduced to this Alien world that I did not know too much about, eventually realizing that it was another excuse that my ego had created to keep itself within its own boundaries, as it did not want to leave its own premise, which offered the security of its own harness. The animal mind of the ego had to vacate, through finding its own strength to leave its own security and move forward into the inner sanctum of the in-known. Hence the Sphinx before the pyramids in Egypt.

This is the era where this word "Star Seed" became more substantially drawn into our vocabulary. When explained through a metaphysical interpretation, we are becoming aware of our inner light and through following many of George's movies, we are able to digest many other factors that tune into the facets that are already placed into our inner regime at the time of gestation, through the supreme consciousness. Our inner self is identical in unison mathematically, to the outer collective. This is when we begin to plant our inner harvest, as we release our information, the language of the stars begin to seed through our education, careers, teachers, parents, and children etc.

I have had many interesting people come for counselling from the highest intellectual minds, to the little one who shortly after birth have the ability to see through the layers of consciousness and who have great difficulties to explain how they deal with this experience. These little ones live their lives alone, where they're happy creating their "Own Friends" as there are no arguments. They become their "Own Council", they form their "Own Government" and they have exalted their mind up into their "Own Royal" behaviour. They are referred to by society as the "Indigo Children". Remember the colour blue, is associated to the throat area of humans, where we form our communication with others and ourselves! Through the inner rainbow, it refracts the colour of our inner Royalty. These children draw upon the intelligence of the brain stem area and the three glands that converge to unite all our senses: hearing, seeing, knowing, speaking, and, notably, the opening of their third or inner eye atop the pineal gland, allowing them to see from within through the frontal lobe of the brain. The challenge faced by teachers is to understand the child and more to the point the teachers have difficulties trying to know how to treat or deal with the child's innocent mind. The training and seminars then began with the teachers, and there were many who wanted to understand this phenomenon. It was new information for them to inherit. They persevered, and it was when they offered assistance to others that I could relax and watch them all extend their own wisdom which changed their vocabulary. I am pleased to say, the majority of the parents were exceedingly proud of their offspring once they understood the mindset of their child, when they were informed of how to deal with the brilliance of their child. Remember with each new generation, there are 20% of the population born with this gift of seeing from within at an early age.

We will move on to explain the educated minds I have encountered. The majority of them held prestigious positions, such as scientists, physicists, engineers, university professors, mathematicians, surgeons, judges, and various others. When they sat down before me, I adjusted my frequencies to see who they were within by requesting a concise life summary in three short sentences. They usually responded promptly and without hesitation.

Remarkably, the common thread among them was an acknowledgement of their solitary nature. The first sentence frequently began with "I am a loner - I don't spend too much time with others, I prefer to be in my own company. I like quiet." As I gazed into their mind's eye, their symbol emerged on their forehead, where we are alerted to whom this person is on an inner level. It is one of the first things we are trained to become aware of. Are they from another planet, or are they ET's, is the gossip out there to the innocent mind.

No, it is nothing so spectacular, it is how their internal mathematics are threaded throughout their DNA during their gestation, to assist them with the opportunity to evolve the family linage or their tribal (family) DNA into a higher resolution of intellect. Through their own hereditary conditioning, this opportunity allows them to lift up the barriers that have restricted the family linage due to embedded fears carried forward through many previous generations. I especially noticed this in Europe where many individuals originated from third-world or war-torn countries.

These individuals excelled in their own education and continued to extend their program beyond their parental upbringing. Moreover, their communication with other members of their personal family, we noticed how other members of the same family were also initiated into following in their footsteps, as this awakening automatically clears the hic-ups of the past. This example has shown us how the previous generations were finally absolved of shame and guilt, so that the current generations could inherit their DNA with a more advanced and substantially clarified mind

***

To conclude this revised book, those of you who have committed yourselves to this next journey of self-discovery, you now know and can accept who you truthfully are – you are an adept of the Laws of the Universe in training, renowned as an ETI, an "Extra-Terrestrial Intellectual in Training." As you advance your mind through your new found belief in Self, your Soul gives you never-ending gifts of knowledge. To believe in yourself takes a tremendous amount of courage, and that courage will lead you into other parallel worlds of existence (metaphorically). Those worlds begin to align within you, which opens up the next continuance mathematically of your stored information in your cells, where you receive new information through you having earned the freedom to use them to promote your tomorrows. Parallel worlds are created from the levels of your intelligence; they are your personalities (aspects of self) co-creating an experience using a different emotion, and they live deep within your auric fields which allows you to have many new opportunities to choose and promote your thinking wisely.

My next endeavour involves writing a book on Body Language. This venture is a meticulous process, as I have approximately 9000 pages to decipher and compile to craft this book step by step. Through my education into discovering how our cellular structure communicates to us moment by moment, this knowledge has opened a doorway to further explain the intricacies of Body Language. Consider why we might itch and scratch, why we rub our eyes, why accidents happen, how we can inadvertently manifest diseases, or even why we get bitten by a mosquito. What thoughts attract these occurrences into our energy? Have you ever listened to the language of the trees and, in particular, the birds that communicate with us throughout the day, often referred to as the earth's angels? Our animal companions are equally fascinating; they seem to possess a profound understanding of us, more so than we have of ourselves. These second-dimensional minds are here to serve us.

I thank you for having the confidence to read my story up to this last page, as I know there are still many of you that are having these experiences in your life. May you all inherit the wind, which is the breath released from the Universal Laws, as they promote and keep us safe in their arms, through us understanding this "Greatest Oracle of the Divine!"

APPENDIX A

My Contact with Extra-Terrestrial Intelligence in a condensed version/time sequence with condensed Metaphysical explanations (including Mayan and Egyptian philosophy).

My own initial contact with Extra-Terrestrial Intelligence (ETI), was in 1977 – on 11 November, to be exact – when they arrived on my property in Australia that evening. I was milking the cows at the usual time, and I had just nestled into the flanks of my favourite cow, Sarah. She liked to be the first one in line and the first into the bales, and she did not like hanging around waiting. We had a special affinity, and, as I communicated with her, she would moan softly to me when she agreed – or snort if she disagreed – with my thinking.

That particular evening, my thoughts were jumbled; I needed this time to be alone to work out where I was up to. The milking of my cows was my meditation at the end of the working day, before I went up to the house to tackle the evening meal, baths, homework, etc. I focused on my hand movements, as I loved to watch the mathematics one used for releasing the milk. I followed my daily mathematics (I reviewed my thoughts of that day) that evening; soon, my rhythm began to pick up, and the milk was flowing in a steady stream into the bucket.

Just then I felt these subtle vibrations up and down my spine. At first, I thought that Jack the snake, must have been close by, but, when I looked around, he wasn't there. Jack was a harmless 3.3-metre-long python that lived in the dairy, and his job was to keep the rats out of the grain bins. When he moved along the rafters and came up close to where I was milking, he would swing down and sway behind me. I could always sense when Jack was behind me. It is amazing how, when our mind is focused and still, our sixth sense just takes over. When that happens, we feel another energy enter our own, and we call this sensation ESP. Feeling this – and how strongly you feel it, if at all – depends on the focus of your mind; that is, whether your mind is working for you. In any case, when I "sensed" Jack, I would squirt some milk up at him, and he would sway down, open his mouth, and have a drink. Jack had a unique energy, it was long and kind of like a groan; it took time for his vibrations to move throughout the length of his whole body.

That night, the vibrations that I was feeling continued up and down my spine, and I relaxed into them. To be honest, at that time, I imagined that it was something between me and Sarah – just the cow and I nurturing one another and becoming one – once I determined that Jack was nowhere around. The next thing I remember was coming to – it seemed like moments later, but I felt like I had been out or away. I looked into a full bucket with five gallons of fluffy milk filled right to the top. I still had the same cow in the bale. I moved the bucket out over against the shed wall and let her out of the bale, explaining to the cow that I was sorry and must have fallen asleep for a few minutes. I felt contentment surge through my body, followed by a sense of peace that I wanted to last forever.

I put the other calves onto their mothers, as I certainly had enough milk to feed the family until the following morning's milking. I opened the gate to let the cows out of the yards, and I noticed three lights bobbing around in the paddock on the other side of our creek. This large creek was the children's swimming hole, as well as our irrigation supply, and it was some 40 metres wide. The lights that I saw appeared about twenty metres on the flat land on the other side of the creck.

My first thought was to wonder why my boys were out there and what they were doing with the pressure lamps. I called out to them, but they did not respond. However, my calling attracted my husband's attention. He was working on a tractor in the large machinery shed nearby, and he came over to me. We were in the middle of another drought at that time, and I said to my husband, "Look at those boys with the pressure lamps! I hope they are careful, as the grass is tinder dry, and we don't need a fire at this time of year." He explained that the boys were up at the house, not over in the paddock, and then he, too, became inquisitive about the lights. He picked up the milk bucket and we went up to the house.

My family had come up from the south to spend Christmas with us, and the house was busy and full of laughter. My husband thought that maybe someone was trying to maverick one of our cows for their own Christmas, so he gathered the men. They constructed a plan as to which way they could surround those people who were so blatantly close to the house with their lights. The women meandered down to the cattle yards and sat up high on the slip rails of the yards, watching as the men came around to block all the entrances.

Off the men went towards the paddock, approaching from different directions in trucks and tractors and on motorbikes. As they approached the area, the three lights lifted up off the ground and hovered above the trees. The men stopped dead in their tracks to view the phenomenon. The lights started dancing around in the sky, but, as my husband walked towards them, they took off over the hill. The men came back to the house in awe of what they had just seen, and we all sat down to one of the quietest evenings that we had shared in a long time.

At that time, I had cervical cancer, which my doctor was treating. However, a few days after that first ETI contact, I came to the realization that my cancer had disappeared. I did not know what had happened or why, but I could feel a gentle lightness within me; I felt different and at peace with myself. Allowing that feeling to just sit with me for a bit, after Christmas, I went back to my doctor. He did some tests, and then he informed me that I was in remission. My mathematics had equalized, and so the old energy no longer had a place to feed from. That healing produced a huge window in my mind, where I received a second opportunity to reshape my thoughts and begin my life again.

For an explanation for this section of the story. Our inner language (mind chatter/thoughts) is a menagerie of egotistical and emotional thoughts that we are forever searching for within ourselves – we search for this in order to understand ourselves. This is the gift that the ancient ones left for us. For example the hieroglyphs of Egypt are explaining the language of the unconscious recognition – of our unconscious (higher) mind, which is our Divine intellect - our highest realm of intellect. Paintings are on the walls in many of the tombs, where we see boats carried along by the High Priests. The number of men supporting the boat informs us about the message; regardless, this boat was referred to as the "Bja-Ark"! The Bja is referred to as "the ego asking questions"; the men who supported it are the High Priests, which are metaphoric symbols of the glands around our throat area. As our intellect opens up, these boats evolve until they become our ship (body) to sail the consciousness. Once we have left our third-dimensional reality, we begin to create our own spaceship.

In reference to the Mayan civilization and the picture of a Mayan at the controls of a supposed – or metaphorical – spaceship is scribed through the metaphysical codes. It is an explanation of how our intelligence releases through the autonomic responses; that is, through the energy of how our Soul (unconscious mind) enables us to intellectually move forward. The intellect of the spaceship was left for us thousands of years ago, through the Mayan heritage. The Mayan Palenque code is similar to the Egyptian King Tutankhamen; they both represent the same states of consciousness, which are explained all the way through their emotional hierarchical languages. The Mayans explained through the left hemisphere of the brain, and the Egyptians explained through the right hemisphere. Symbolism is the doorway that creates our reality; everything we walk towards in our future has been repeated every day since human existence began! As we evolve into our own structure of intelligence, we all symbolically build and collect our "ship of light" – consequentially, all of this pertains to the result of our unconscious education.

Take note that the Great Pyramid in Egypt had four ships buried at each of its corners, which relate to the four directions or Medicine Wheel that we use. Those ships represent the temple of how we earn our freedom to sail into the consciousness. The consciousness represents the worlds of thoughts instilled in our brain. Do you see how Homer explained the journey aboard the ship in the

Odyssey (the ode to Zeus)? Maybe now you can bring together the story of how, once we face our self, the Extra-Terrestrial Intelligence of our mind begins to export itself back through the cellular recognition of our body.

To continue. The lights made contact again two years later (in 1979) at my daughter's engagement party. Through my belief and the growth that I had given to myself, I had completed the next stage of the program designed on my behalf in order to my benefit and satisfaction. As the guests danced into the night, those three bright lights appeared, dancing in the sky to the beat of our music. We had invited 120 people that evening, and this phenomenon stunned them all. They laughed and cheered at the movement of those lightships swaying in the night sky.

My husband and a friend went towards them, and, whoosh! The lights disappeared very quickly over the hill and out of sight. As you can imagine, it took us quite a while to get back to dancing! That second contact took away any remaining fear that I harboured as to Extra-Terrestrial Intelligence.

The lessons I earned this time were in regard to my having to disconnect from my daughter, as she had chosen to create a new life and was about to be introduced into another tribe/family. She was now becoming my emotional age, and her thoughts were focusing on her new life and future. I say that my daughter was my "emotional age", as she had now become a woman who was learning to experience her own freedom in order to begin her next inherited mind.

I went on to rear my other children to adulthood, and then I became emotionally driven to begin my quest for knowledge. My life changed rapidly. I, the student, was ready; thus, the teachers began to appear, placed before me to explain the things that I did not understand.

In the late '80s and early '90s, I watched as metaphysically my own body formed the reconstruction of a ship of light. It began with a vision of a rowboat coming into the shore through a mist; at the helm, was a big blue bird that I now understand to have represented the Egyptian God P'tah, and, at the rudder, was an old man directing the boat onto the beach. First, I constructed my small rowboat, which, over time, grew into a magnificent galleon that became an ocean liner. Next began the journey of my body, representing a train, bus, motorbike, car, tractor, etc.; with each one of those evolutions, in turn, representing the energy of my personalities (aspects of self) in motion, working with the earth. Originally, the Universe delivered the earth to us as our body, which we could rely on to support us. Through the Laws of Shamanism, I understood that all this was here to serve us, replacing in us what we did not have – and, perhaps still do not have – the inner strength to accomplish. Our inner totem was constructing itself through the evolution of the technology that we have gratefully accomplished and achieved to be of service to the planet at this time. My last step began with planes – from a little crop duster that removed the irritations of the mind, to a helicopter, an airbus, a jumbo jet, a stealth bomber, a rocket ship, a satellite – and, finally, the space station! My dreams and visions revealed all to me; if I did not understand each individual message, the story had to begin all over again. That is when the creation of the spaceship began; it has taken many years to construct itself, and it is still in the making to this day – I am permanently rewarded as I unravel the codes, in my quest for knowledge.

At the beginning of our quest, we are introduced to the side of the world that is opposite from our own. It is through this attainment that we humans can reach our future without the dilemmas that we create along the way. Many people, when coming into the connection of self with an enquiring mind, have an urge to take a journey to Egypt, Tibet, China, Japan, or India. We have an urge to reach out away from our homeland. Why? We need to search for our opposite; maybe we have a desire to taste the unknown and stretch our boundaries to see how far we can go. And then we must begin to connect with the four corners – from the south to the north, and from the west to the east – that is the square becoming the circle, in which we search for information regarding the Medicine Wheel, which represents the Collective Consciousness.

In the beginning of my journey, I tried four times to go to India and Tibet with friends who wanted to return to the wisdom of the other side of the world; it never eventuated for me. Either my car would not start, as the battery became mysteriously flat, and so I missed my plane; or I got to the airport, but there wasn't a seat available for me. The same experience kept on repeating itself. The Universe delivered a message for me in all this, of course, as to why I could not attend those countries. I began to realize that I had to find the answers within me, and so I humbly apologized for my behaviour and began again. I listened to my friends' descriptions when they returned, and I found that I could learn and understand their stories by finding my own answers within myself. Now I am free to travel the planet, and, in each country that I journey to, I know that I am as they are. I am treated like "royalty" when I enter other lands, and I reciprocate accordingly.

From there, I went into the journey head-on, full of praise for myself and wonderment at what my possibilities were; my yearning for self had moved me forward. The healing worlds opened up, and into them I swam, learning many different modalities and realizing that each one advanced a step past the other!

In my quest of knowledge I found that the Collective Consciousness could also be referred to as the Collective Inner Science. In other words, this inner science explains how the outer science shaped itself; we understand our self through understanding those who have walked before us and by understanding them, we come to understand our Self – and the Universe – even more. I had difficulties in understanding and accepting that the word science ("science") is created through the acceptance of balancing the energy of the Collective, and that Collective creates the essence of the microscopic worlds, which, in turn, create the macrocosmic evolution.

Remember that the definitions of this planet are an illusion, looking at the illusion, creating the illusion, collecting the illusion, for the illusion. No matter what happens in your life, it is all meant to be at that given time; it must happen to you just as it happens – until you become that end illusion that you are so busily creating, all by yourself. That final illusion is your "Vision World" – or your "Vision Quest" – it is where you become the source of your own knowing. It is only four little words, which, through the codes, interpret as, "your truth releases through understanding your Soul". In order for you to manifest your future, you learn to become the illusion of self. You automatically become that outer auric field; all of which creates a vibration that collects your future on your behalf. The more we become that permanent mirror – or outer boundary of self – the higher we extend our intellect; that boundary is the light of your own creation, which is urged up to become the cap on your pyramid. It is the outer boundary that collects your strength. It must equalize with your inner thoughts.

How do we become our own illusion? We have learned that our left brain is our ego, and our right brain is our emotions, according to the sacred language. This has been explained to me through my understanding the hidden codes of the Bible, which was written in a language explaining the evolution of our unconscious mind. We train our ego to look at our emotions, and, in return, those emotions mirror back to us. When we understand all this information, the autonomic responses of our nervous system help to ascend us to the next level. This governing of self is what we are all about – it is not the two brains melding, rather, it is the two separate entities walking the same path. The illusion is created through the equality of both brains walking hand-in-hand with one another, which then becomes our intellectual light.

Both brains evolve to a certain level, where each can view the other in balance; at that point, the reflection begins to manifest. This then becomes the Higher Self – or the "Royal Order" of things to come. That order is what we refer to as our "Godhead" and this is where we open ourselves up into the pineal gland. Through our thoughts coming together, we balance our energy, where our light becomes the reflection of the two hemispheres of our brain. The Higher Self is freed from the ego's restrictions, as it learns to harmonically balance and extend itself. As we reach up, we find that we are able to look down at the same time.

To explain further, our intellectual light manifests only when the mind is focused. When the ego (or conscious mind) releases, through learning to trust itself, it is then collected into the subconscious (or emotional mind), and the emotional mind automatically trusts the next level, which is the unconscious mind (or Higher Self). You cannot doubt yourself for a moment! When you first begin to reach up into the heavens, it is a step by step introduction, where your Higher Self begins speaking through you. It is autonomically tuning you in to the right frequencies in order to prepare you for the Collective to come through loud and clear. Your body awakens and releases to let the force fields speak. Thus, your respectful light shines through you having earned yourself! In the same way that an astronaut is plugged into the oxygen from his spacecraft, so, too, are we plugged into the Collective? That light is your intelligence, and you create and release your freedom through accepting it. Please remember that your light comes through the power of love, not through the love of power.

The Extra-Terrestrial Intelligence returned again in 1991, twelve years after its last appearance in my life (during my daughter's engagement party). This event in 1991 occurred one night after 120 days of my being in a trance-like state; during that time, I had talked to hundreds of people who knocked on my door, twenty-four hours a day. Throughout these previous days, I had to learn to become an open trance channel, where I seemed to have become robotic in all of my endeavours. I was permanently plugged into the Collective Consciousness; I could hear and relate to all of it, but I still tried to go about my own business at the same time.

People walked through my house, day and night; I did not even know most of them. They wanted to listen, share, ask questions, or be healed; they were searching for answers to their own pent-up emotions. To begin with, it was just the local people, and then it expanded to people from different areas of the state and all over the country; after a while, they started to come from other countries, near and far. They all just wanted to share their stories with someone who understood. I never sent an invitation, so how did they know where I lived? Their unconscious mind, unknown to their conscious selves, had directed them to my house.

Every moment of my life released a new wisdom to add to the

words of my inner dictionary. The worlds of healing create an extreme religious experience in the self. I found that I was being brought up into the higher Shamanic resonances of what we refer to as "psychic surgery". This level awakens in us when we have connected in totality with the unconscious mind. My life had totally changed forever. I could feel a conclave of eclectic experiences working with me, and I knew that I would never return to the old me – in other words, my excuses were a thing of the past. My inner clarity reigned supreme.

On that night, after 120 days in my trance-like state, my students walked in with smiles on their faces, asking what I had been up to. They said that they could see my home very clearly from a distance, as it had a large ball of light around it that seemed to glow in the dark. I had up to twenty students who came to my home every week for meditation and communication. We settled down, I gave my meditation, they asked their questions, and I answered them. The topic for that evening was "Relationship"; on that particular night, time just slipped away.

Suddenly, we heard two knocks on the front door, so one of my students got up and opened it; nobody was there. As soon as he had closed the door and sat down again, we heard two knocks on the back door; again, nobody was there. The students thought that somebody was playing games with us. After a long moment, we heard two more knocks on the front door, and another student quickly opened it. To our surprise, a mist came rolling through the open door, and we saw eleven Aliens coming through the mist and into my lounge room.

Of the eleven, ten were short, and one was tall. The time was 11:11 p.m., and it was 11 November 1991 (11-11-1991). Remember that my first ETI experience happened on 11-11-1977. I had not prepared this image myself; through the layers of my own thinking in my trance like confinement, my energy had collected, reached up and connected with the highest form of the Collective Consciousness.

Only three of us in that group could see the holographic image of the Aliens (ETI), as we had all become ensconced into the fourth dimension through understanding their vibrational thinking. Some of the other students could only see the mist, as their fear, which had not yet abated, had already taken control of their thinking. The newer students just rolled over and went to sleep. Their mind barriers had jumped to attention as soon as the mist entered the room, and the phenomenon had blocked their inner sight. You only fear for yourself. Remember, please: If you think it, you create it, and then it will become!

The tallest Alien told me that his name was "Pharaohtriea" and he came through into my world. He explained that he was a member of the "Brotherhood of Light" which I had never heard of; he told me that they were all from a planet of emerald-green situated in the eastern galaxies. Their emerald-green planet was next to the blue planet. Their home was a planet of hope, love, and service – who could fear that? I later understood that the colour of emerald-green represented my emotional self. On the Medicine Wheel and in the principles of Shamanism, the east symbolically represents the worlds within. Pharaohtriea was tall, light, and so very gentle; he communicated to me with compassion and love. I felt that emotion course through every cell in my body. I call him a "male energy", as he spoke to me in a low, melodious, masculine voice. He said, "Have no fear; I mean no harm to you. I am as you are. You and I are of same mind in this moment, and, with your trust in me, we can be one." He smiled. As his small mouth moved, I felt the subtle energy flow throughout my body. I felt comfortable, as his vibration was so calm. "When you can find your faith in me, as I have in you, we will then have the opportunity to communicate as one," he said.

The group became quiet and subdued. They looked to one another in anticipation, and, through their support of each other, their fear began to relax. Although they still could not see, they could feel the energy in the room change to a gentle coolness. The entrance of these beings into my home had made a great difference to the inside temperature. It was a hot 35 degrees Celsius outside, but now the students were looking for blankets to wrap themselves in. They had placed their shock around them for protection, so their fear was in attendance. I realized that the Collective Consciousness was preparing me for another paradigm shift in my own consciousness; as always, I became a willing subject. I had been waiting in anticipation for this since 1979 – finally! – my moment had come. I asked Pharaohtriea why he was there, and he explained that I was ready to evolve and receive my next shift of consciousness. I was more than ready. The last 120 days had been, literally, mind-blowing; I had moved into realms of thought that I could have never created through my own thinking. What more could I expect? I had let this loving feeling flow through me, and I never wanted it to cease!

Pharaohtriea asked for and received permission to speak to the group. He and I both adjusted our energies, and he then proceeded to speak to the group through me. I didn't panic; I just allowed him entry, finding him to be an easy and gentle energy to blend with. His voice was quiet; his breath was gentle, and it tasted of the crispness of the high mountains. I smelt the essence of the fir trees. It felt like I was communicating with someone in a dream.

After introducing himself to them, he explained that he was a consciousness for the next opportunity that was available to all of humanity, and, when they had enough faith in themselves, they could learn from him. He said that every human with a yearning to learn more about him/herself has the opportunity to evolve into this next step of understanding; furthermore, he explained that, when the time was right for each of them, it would automatically begin to shape into their own consciousness. Pharaohtriea delivered a message about attachments in relationships, and when finished he thanked me for my participation, and then he gently withdrew his energy.

The other ten beings walked around and the room filled with laughter at their antics; they subtly touched the students who could not see them, yet could sense – or feel – their energy. After a while, the mist gently left the room, and we watched as it disappeared through the keyhole of the front door. A subtle silence filled the room, and no one moved. We all had been completely unprepared for this event. The temperature began to rise again, and those students whom the energy shift had put to sleep began to stir. My students floated out the door that night and were never the same again. They spoke about that experience for months, realizing that they had been shown the opportunity to create their own time.

When Pharaohtriea returned three days later, I was alone; that is when my new life with him began. I found that total seclusion was going to be the only way for me to adjust to this time warp without the interference of others. I felt safe and comfortable with my exalted friend who showed me an immense respect; and, the more interested and preoccupied I became with his teachings, the more contented I felt. As I began to accept my new awakening to this knowledge, I changed Pharaohtriea's name to "the Architect". That name re-entered my psyche from my childhood. This "Being of Light" reminded me of the story of Moses, and I had learned as a child that he was the Architect of Egypt.

So, in reflection to the story; for 120 days I had been working in a trance-like state and was permanently plugged into the Collective Consciousness. My heart was open through the power of love. I reached a pinnacle/peak in my thinking; my conscious mind and subconscious mind were in unison and entered the unconscious mind (highest intellect or Higher Self). My students had seen a light (my intellectual light), surrounding my house when they had arrived. My Higher Self was showing me the next step in my evolution - into Extra Terrestrial Intelligence (Universal intelligence).

Remember the emerald-green planet represented my emotional self and the eastern galaxies represented the worlds within - the worlds within me. The 'White Brotherhood' the Collective Consciousness. Pharaohtriea stated; "When you can find your faith in me, as I have in you, we will then have the opportunity to communicate as one." In other words; I with trust in myself will forever be one/total awareness of my 'Higher Self' - always working with the Collective Consciousness.

The Collective Consciousness was providing the paradigm shift in my own consciousness. I then worked with Pharaohtriea until I had completed the paradigm shift within myself.

The Journey continued. As the months rolled by, information filled me constantly, with each bit always filtering through one after the other, as it all added to the value of my inner dictionary, which I now realized was part of the Collective Consciousness. One day, I was asked to prepare myself to move on from that area by the ocean; as my next place of importance emerged, I had to learn to detach from the place that had educated me and that I had grown to love. I allowed myself to accept the direction I received, which was to go out into the west to live on a cattle property – 540 square kilometres of beautiful land in the Australian Outback, four of the world's most wonderful people already living there. And so I found myself living in a tin shed on the property that had been revealed to me; it was far enough away from the homestead that I could live and work in detachment, but not so far away that I was totally isolated from all of humanity.

Three light ships worked with me during my time in the Australian Outback. Those ships were the Collective Consciousness mirroring and reflecting back to me through my channels (emotional intelligence channels), letting me know that I was okay. They gave me the chance to discover my own discernment, where I could find the faith and courage to go on. I had to believe in those lessons; I needed to see a form of logical consciousness, and, if I went out too far, those lights gave me the confidence to come back into my reality. I had to expel through my own consciousness what a spaceship or UFO was, and how it built up its own sequences to move in a holographic manner throughout this planet.

I learned to manifest time and move through my own future in order to see what I could create in a metaphor. I found that my body was evolving into geometric shapes, or beings; at first, I thought these from another planet, but they weren't – they were within my own aura. Those beings were reflections of my own thoughts, thinking in their emotional depth of time and reflecting back to me. This is what we refer to as a "time warp"'.

In humans, time warps through our own energies vibrating at a faster rate, which symbolically creates the strength for the ego to coincide with itself. When we do not understand this, it gathers back into itself and blocks our energy, which then becomes the next step of our fear, and we know that this is the forerunner to all our dis-eases. The inner realms give us the gift of achieving our reality. My totem power was coming alive. I was like an astronaut shuddering through the gravity fields of the planet.

Throughout this exalted time, I watched the manifestation of one of my thoughts, seeing how it worked and evolved itself through my billions of cells to create that starship – or UFO. I watched how the inner light created itself, through the conductive electricity of my brain which freely passed throughout my nervous system. I watched as my thoughts changed, each one attracting the next. It was also interesting to note, how my thoughts presented themselves in so many different shapes and sizes. Which one was important? Which one could rely on its self? Which one had to expand and grow in order to able to sustain its self and not look for others to support it? I watched how the mathematics of the mind created the symbol, and then how that symbol changed as an emotion filtered through to form the next thought. I was watching how our consciousness created its own collective energy, which, in turn, created our reality.

I also learned that we never came from another planet; it is all happening right here on Planet Earth – or, "UR-T", which, through the metaphysical codes, means "understanding and releasing the truth". We can take "UR-T" to the next level of consciousness and decode "EA-R-TH", which means "through my energy ascending, I release the truth from heaven".

These Beings of Light that presented themselves to me took on hideous shapes and sizes, at times; I still had to communicate with them, even though I sometimes felt that I was in the parking lot of a science fiction movie. I had to take note of the shape of their hands and feet, the shape of their heads, the warp in their spines, the way they walked, etc. Over time, I realized that they were vibrations of consciousness that had already evolved and that represented the emotional difficulties they had evolved into in order to digest what they were thinking. I was receiving their life force as to how they had continually gestated through their emotional upheaval of not understanding themselves. They were representing the genetic vibration that they had inherited. These same entities were also the personalities that all humans create within themselves when the mind is out of balance.

I was learning to communicate with other species that had already evolved from the ocean; I discovered how they had prepared and earned their own evolution, through recording a balance to their understanding of what the Collective had relayed back to them. The majority of them were androgynous, through their positive behaviour evolving up into the unconscious mind. One of the most important species to me was the insect population; I understood that they read combustible energy through living totally in their evolution, which is equivalent to our unconscious mind. These were the worlds of the Extra-Terrestrial Consciousness; their hideous shapes and sizes were magnified through the awakening of my inner eye, as I received the creative reality that conducted their consciousness.

I was manifesting a large hologram, and I realized that I was working with the eternal energy. There were the faces of the stick creatures, the eyes of the fly, the head of the ant, and the blur of the wings of the cricket. I was living a re-enactment of the evolution of the human brain; this is the myth, which is one of the highest levels that create the largest facet of the geometry of the Universe. Those years of terror and anxiety all came together over the next few years, as I climbed out of the bottomless pit to discover that I had the sustainability to reverse everything that I had been taught. If I reversed everything, I could see how the manifestation had formed.

My next education began in earnest, in order to introduce me into the world of pneumatic waves of consciousness, which I already had begun to gather around me. Eventually these waves took on the shapes of people who appeared to walk through walls, one at a time, and then stand before me or sit on the bed beside me. To my state of mind, at that time, those people were complete in their holographic form, and they seemed real; as if they were physically there. I realized that I had intellectually entered into the light worlds – somewhere between matter and antimatter – so, again, I trusted these experiences, and I moved on.

One Soul who came to teach me had an aura of colourful energy that resonated around him for about 1.5 meters. Those brightly coloured energy sparkled and moved as he spoke. This fascinated me in the beginning, because, as he spoke his words, they never collided with the colours of the waves; the sounds and colours seemed to move in harmonic unison, as if their own movement reinforced them.

As this brightly coloured one came to the end of his conversation, more Beings of Light were attracted into my peripheral vision. It seemed that the next one was magnetically pulled towards me, and the one who had just finished was automatically pushed back. These incoming and outgoing auric energies travelled in a curve, seeming to circumnavigate the energy mathematically so as to determine in which direction to move. The polarity shifts of positive and negative were at work here, and I watched in continual fascination. I felt like a magnet that attracted these energies according to the resonation of the mathematics of my own emotional value at that time.

This is only a small percentage of what happened in my life at that time, as everything seemed to be shown to me in an instant. My mind had gone beyond its own value of time, and every lesson was given to me in the blink of an eye. Please enjoy your journey at every step.

Your Notes:

Books By O.M. Kelly (Omni)

Decoding The Mind Of God
Author O.M. Kelly's seminal work, "Decoding the Mind of God", is a compilation of nine volumes of metaphysical information based on the research into the coded information of the Laws of the Universe, also known as the Collective Consciousness, and represents a groundbreaking contribution to our understanding of the metaphysical universe. Now, all nine volumes are being released as separate, revised books, each offering a unique perspective on the universe's workings. Omni's work has been widely acclaimed for its depth of insight, and her contributions to the field of metaphysics have been groundbreaking.

The nine separate volumes encompassing:

The Laws of the Universe
Thought
Dis-Ease
Death
Sexuality and Spirituality
The Dolphin's Breath
Sacred Alphabet and Numerology
Sacred Fung Shwa
Extra-Terrestrial Intelligence.

Updated version of each book now being released separately.

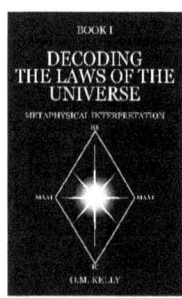

Book I. Decoding The Laws Of The Universe
If you're looking to unlock the hidden potential within you and transform your life, "Decoding the Laws of the Universe" is the book for you. This powerful and insightful book is designed to help you understand the deeper, metaphysical aspects of life and tap into the transformative power of the universe utilising the secrets of our Individual Universal Law.

This book serves to introduce you into the secrets of our Individual Universal Law. This amazing knowledge and wisdom, is transformative on a personal level and creates the opportunity for you to interrelate with the Laws of the Universe. Throughout this book, you will dive deep into the inner workings of your mind and discover the hidden laws that govern your life. You will learn about the alchemy of the mind and how to harness its power to create positive change in your life and the world around you. Through the lens of Metaphysical philosophy, you will gain a new perspective on the world and your place in it. You will learn how the universe communicates with you through coded intelligence and how to unlock the hidden messages that are all around you.

This book is a journey for personal transformation and spiritual growth. Take a voyage of exploration of the expansive vistas of information discovering the codes of Metaphysics and the Quest of Life. You will learn the Metaphysical coded wisdom of the ancients for the necessary mind elements to transit into a higher mindset. Explore the secret relationship between the Earth and human beings, the higher mind, the Metaphysical journey, the importance of self, belief in self, the codes of mythology, a higher level of attainment, releasing the past, fears and evolving one's light on a Metaphysical level, what causes stress, work place promotion and why it does not happen, and many other topics. Included is a short overview of the conventional Twelve Laws of the Universe.

Book II. Decoding Thought
Welcome to a journey of self-discovery and exploration of the mysteries of the universe. "Decoding Thought" is a ground-breaking book that explores the power of the mind and the principles of metaphysical thought. Through a deep exploration of the mind and body connection, the author provides readers with insights to unlock the full potential of their thoughts. This book provides a guide to harnessing the power of the mind to create the life you desire. With explanations of metaphysical principles, the book makes these often complex concepts accessible to readers. "Decoding Thought" takes you on a journey through the vast landscape of the human mind. Explore the mysteries of thought power, and how it can shape our reality and transform our lives. The power of thought is not just a theoretical concept. It is a tangible force that can be harnessed to bring about significant changes in our lives.

This book can expand your consciousness and open your mind to new possibilities. By exploring the metaphysical principles that underlie our existence, you can gain a new perspective on life and the world around you. This book provides through a metaphysical interpretation explanations into the various aspects of thought power, including how it is linked to our DNA, and the roles played by the pituitary and pineal glands in our thought processes. O.M. Kelly also explains the metaphysical language in reference to the codes of the Egyptian Philosophies, the Bible, myths, cultures, and how they connect to the power of thought. The journey continues with a deep dive into the inner Secret School of Metaphysics, where we discover the Alchemy of the Brain and the pathway to our truth. Discover the unconscious/higher mind, and our Life Quest, which opens the doors to the Psychometric Consciousness. Through the lens of metaphysical interpretation, you will gain a new perspective on the impact of thought on our mental and emotional states that includes a look at Depression, Coping with Change and how to retrain our brain patterns to be positive and moving forward for our Financial Abundance and manifesting prosperity. The book ends with a brief overview of the brain/mind, and a short Q&A on thought power. This metaphysical book on the power of thought is a guide to discovering your true potential and creating the life you desire.

"Decoding Thought" is a must-read for anyone seeking to unlock the full potential of their mind and harness the power of the universe to create a life of fulfilment and this book serves as an invaluable resource.

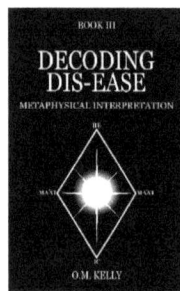

Book III. Decoding Dis-Ease

Introducing "Decoding Dis-Ease" a Metaphysical Interpretation into understanding the intricate web of factors that contribute to our health and well-being. From the author of several groundbreaking works on the interaction of the mind and body, this book delves into a wide range of topics related to dis-ease. It is a fascinating and insightful book that offers a fresh perspective on health and healing. It is a must-read for anyone interested in the mind-body connection.

Readers will be inspired to embark on a quest of discovering the codes within themselves, recognizing that every cell in our body is pure Cosmic Consciousness. They will also gain a deeper understanding of specific health topics such as the thyroid, the kidneys, men's problems, and many other topics from a Metaphysical perspective. The book also examines how a dis-ease is given to us in group energy and the complex interplay between our bodies and minds, and how every human has the consequences of all that we do and experience.

Book IV. Decoding Death

Looking for a thought-provoking exploration of death and the afterlife? Look no further than O.M. Kelly's book, "Decoding Death".

"Decoding Death takes us on a transformative Metaphysical journey through the mysteries of the Universe. O.M. Kelly—known as Omni—provides an expanded horizon of possibilities, awareness, and a transformative perspective. In this book, Omni delves into a wide range of topics related to dying and death, from the loss of a loved one to a viewing of the afterlife. Omni has a unique ability to view the Laws of the Universe using her extraordinary state of heightened awareness and multi-dimensional perception and through the lens of metaphysics offers a unique perspective on the nature of death and what it means for the human experience.

Omni shares personal experiences and stories, including the passing of her late husband, brother, and parents, and offers a metaphysical insight for those dealing with loss and grief. She explores the transformational process of death and the potential for spiritual growth and enlightenment. The book explains that the human experience of death is part of a larger Universal process that is ultimately guided by a higher intelligence referred to as God (Laws of the Universe/Collective Consciousness) or whatever name you prefer. Omni's exploration of death is both metaphysically comprehensive and thought-provoking, offering readers a deep and nuanced understanding of one of life's greatest mysteries. With chapters on the Three Doorways—Three Stages of Death, The Quantum Hologram—Why a partner dies for the other partner to progress in the "Journey of Life", The Passing to the Afterlife, and many other enlightening chapters, "Decoding Death" offers a unique viewpoint. By drawing on a range of religious, philosophical, and metaphysical perspectives, Omni offers a compelling vision of the human experience of death and its role in the larger Universal Law.

Book V. Decoding Sexuality And Spirituality

Welcome to "Decoding Sexuality and Spirituality" by O.M. Kelly. In this book, explore the fascinating relationship between our sexuality and spirituality, and how these two aspects of ourselves are intimately intertwined. Delve into the concept that sexuality is the doorway to our spirituality, and examine the powerful and transformative energy that is generated when we fully embrace our sexual selves. The book also explores the notion of the metaphysical orgasmic cloud, and how it can be used to deepen our connection to our spiritual selves. We will also examine the role of marriage in our sexual and spiritual lives.

For women, the book offers a unique perspective on the journey of embracing sexuality and spirituality, as well as insights into the different stages of life and how they impact our sexual and spiritual selves. Drawing on both ancient wisdom traditions and metaphysical mythology, the book examines the myth of Hercules and how it relates to our sexual intelligence. By decoding the symbolism of this myth, we can gain a deeper understanding of the ways in which our sexuality and spirituality intersect and influence each other. So if you are ready to embark on a journey of self-discovery and unlock the true potential of your sexual and spiritual selves, then "Decoding Sexuality and Spirituality" is the book for you.

VI. Decoding The Dolphin's Breath

"Decoding The Dolphin's Breath" by O.M. Kelly (Omni) is a captivating exploration of the relationship between humans and dolphins. The book begins with a poignant account of a real-life encounter between the author and a group of wild dolphins, setting the stage for a deep dive into the spiritual and metaphysical significance of dolphins. This captivating book takes readers on a journey into the heart of the dolphin-human relationship, exploring the ways in which these majestic creatures can help us attune to the power of free will, and telepathic communication.

Throughout the Laws of Shamanism the wonderful Dolphin in consciousness, represents the attainment we can reach through ourselves earning our freedom of will. This book explains the benefits of the dolphins breath—the why and how we use the breath that influences our divine mentality. Further, it's a story which reveals how the dolphins have taught us the process to be free of fear, and to tap into the Language of Babylon—to understand the language of Earth. One of the key themes of the book is the idea that dolphins are always breathing their total freedom of thought, and the author provides insights into how humans can learn from this remarkable trait. The book also invites readers to embark on a journey into understanding the telepathic communication of whales and dolphins. Inclusive in the book is a written meditation which assists you to connect to the external consciousness and release the fear that you have wrapped around yourself for protection.

Overall, this book offers a unique and fascinating perspective on the metaphysics of dolphins, and will appeal to anyone interested in spirituality, and the power of the mind.

Book VII. Decoding The Sacred Alphabet And Numerology

This book offers a myriad of explanations concerning the higher consciousness in relationship to names, places and numbers. "Decoding The Sacred Alphabet & Numerology" by O.M. Kelly (Omni) is a thought-provoking and enlightening read that

offers a unique perspective on the metaphysical world of letters and numbers.

Omni's insights and teachings are sure to inspire readers to deepen their understanding of the ancient sacred codes to names of places, your name and the sacred alphabet. The author also delves into the practice of metaphysical numerology, which involves using numerical values to interpret personality traits, life paths, and other aspects of a person's life. Omni explains how metaphysical numerology can be used to gain insight into our spiritual path and to better understand our purpose in life. Your ability to decipher the Sacred Alphabet and Numerology codes commonly and constantly presented to you throughout your life, will open opportunities to expand your consciousness and awareness you never thought possible.

Embark on a journey through the myth of Babylon and Shambhala and discover the sacred language that connects us all. Explore Luxor, the Delta Giza Saqqara and Faiyum, and Solomon's Temple, and uncover the mysteries of Akhenaton and Tomb KV-63. Find out how to unravel the threads of your DNA and unlock the ancient knowledge of the Old Aramaic Story of Aladdin and the Lamp. Explore Grecian stories through the Metaphysical language and travel along the Old Silk Road. Discover the Shamanic inheritance of numbers and their meanings, and learn how we rely on numbers to read the hidden language of the universe. Join O.M. Kelly on a journey of self-discovery and uncover the divine language within.

Book VIII. Decoding Sacred Fung Shwa

Introducing "Decoding Sacred Fung Shwa", the revolutionary guide to understanding and harnessing the energy within your home and yourself. In this book, author O.M. Kelly (Omni), has introduced a metaphysical sixth element that takes our understanding of energy to the next level. By incorporating "Your Life Force," we gain deeper insight into the connection between our homes and our emotional well-being. Discover the power of Fung Shwa and learn how to use it to create a balanced and harmonized environment that supports your mind, body, and Soul.

The book explains the meaning of Sacred Fung Shwa to the Shamanistic principles that underpin it. Delve into the metaphysical medicine wheel and explore the elements of life, before moving on to practical applications of Fung Shwa in the home.

Learn how to visualize your home as a collective energy and clear the clutter to enhance its flow. Discover your Astrological colours and how they can be used in Fung Shwa design, from the kitchen to the bedroom and beyond. Explore the compatibility of personal colours in relationships, and discover the power of paintings, pictures, and mirrors to enhance your home's energy.

But Fung Shwa isn't just about the home—we also explore its applications in the office environment and in small retail businesses. Learn how to apply Fung Shwa principles to a clothing store, shoe store, or café, even discover the role of Fung Shwa in money, and to Metaphysical Numerology.

Throughout it all, we focus on the quest of life and how Fung Shwa can help you achieve your goals and live your best life. So what are you waiting for? Dive into the world of Fung Shwa and transform your home, your business, and your life today!

Book IX. Decoding Extra-Terrestrial Intelligence
Are you ready to embark on a journey of self-discovery? Look no further than O.M. Kelly's groundbreaking book, Book IX "Decoding Extra-Terrestrial Intelligence". Through metaphysical interpretation, O.M. Kelly (Omni) has unlocked the secrets of the universe and revealed that the key to our next step in human evolution lies within ourselves. This book will show you how to tap into the indelible imprint of holographic importance that is seeded within every human, and unleash the Extra-Terrestrial Intelligence that resides within you. Omni shares her own personal journey of encountering Beings of Light and how it has transformed her understanding of the universe and humanity's place within it.

Omni presents the concept that we all have Extra-Terrestrial Intelligence, and have the ability to tap into the vast knowledge and secrets of the universe. The ancient civilizations left behind clues and teachings about this metaphysical existence and it is up to us to continue to uncover and advance the way we think. Through this journey of life, we can unlock the secrets of our own consciousness and tap into the full potential of our existence. This is a fascinating exploration of the mysteries of the universe and the potential for our own personal evolution.

Readers who are interested in self-transformation through universal truths, Metaphysical exploration for personal growth and a journey of self-discovery would be interested in reading this insightful book on contact with Beings of Light and Extra-terrestrial Intelligence, exploring ancient civilizations and the knowledge they possessed about the universe and the human mind.

Power Thought for the Day Oracle Book

"Power Thought For The Day Oracle Book" provides insights to assist you on your life path. Through the "Totem" energy of all, the ancient species that have evolved before us, represent an emotional inheritance that we can rely on to sustain the moment. Each species that has evolved on this planet is recorded into our cellular memory. This book with 22 Major Arcana Shamanic Power Animal Totems provides a contemporary metaphysical interpretation symbolic of our evolution. By selecting a page of the book the Shamanic animal will provide an insight in how you are thinking at this moment in time. Through the contemporary Laws of Shamanism (with a metaphysical interpretation), O.M. Kelly (Omni) has produced a book that will assist the "Path of the Initiate" in emotional intelligence when our mind is in the field of doubt. When we become aware of how we are thinking it is a catalyst for transformation. This compact little book is a handy 4 x 7 inches or 10.2 x 17.8 cm to fit into your pocket or handbag.

How to use the book:
Our higher mind has no time; it steps into and works on behalf of the thought of the moment. This book encompasses 22 Major Totem Power representations, symbolic of our evolution. Close your eyes and inhale and exhale a deep breath and relax and allow yourself no thought as you select the right page of the Shamanic animal presented in this book. The right page will always appear for you at the right moment and you will discover how the power animals are working with you for insight into their wisdom. Different power animals come into our lives at various phases offering messages to guide us on our path.

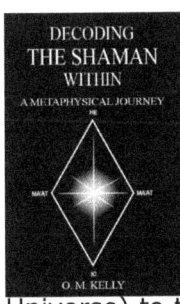

Decoding the Shaman Within

In "Decoding the Shaman Within" international author O.M. Kelly (Omni) shares her Shamanic metaphysical journey. It would be termed a contemporary Shamanic initiation journey; a powerful spiritual enlightenment and transformational voyage of discovering the codes of Metaphysics and the Quest of Life. Through the sacred passage of time Omni discovered the secret codes of the Collective Consciousness (Laws of the Universe) to trek a higher level of consciousness. Throughout

Omni's training to receive the breath of Shamanism, many Elders from other cultures came to Australia and initiated her into their own tribal laws. Most of these Elders were men who arrived on Omni's doorstep uninvited but had received the call from the Universe to pass on their knowledge. Those magnificent people who had also earned their Shamanic experiences, only stayed long enough to give Omni their gift of consciousness and to initiate her into a new Shamanic name, which their tribe had bestowed, and then they disappeared out of Omni's life as quickly as they had come into it.

The Shamanic path in a Metaphysical perspective is the oldest pathway of the tribal law through the evolution of humanity. The Shaman is trained in the ancient language that is instilled in every genetic code that humanity carries within their DNA; you either have the opportunity to open it up and use it, or you just don't bother and choose to ignore it! It is as simple as that!

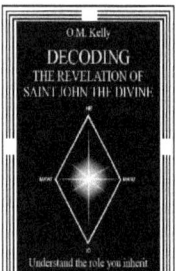

Decoding the Revelation of Saint John the Divine: Understand the role you inherit
The amazing breakthrough book "Decoding the Revelation of Saint John the Divine: Understand the role you inherit", is for anyone with an open, inquiring mind, seeking answers to the surreal descriptions of Earth's final days.

Through years of research O.M. Kelly interprets the cryptology behind the codes of mythology and various religions and has Metaphysically interpreted how the Holy Bible had been written through the original codex of Egyptology. The biblical stories were collected and condensed through the educated minds of that time.

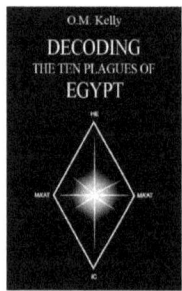

Decoding the Ten Plagues of Egypt
"Decoding the Ten Plagues of Egypt" presents a fresh insight into understanding the hidden structure of the language of how the Bible was written. The reader is introduced to the step by step Metaphysical decoding of the mystifying language, regarding the plagues from the Book of Exodus, Chapters: 7-12 in the Bible.

For the first time in contemporary history the essence of the Book of Exodus and its previously unsolved intriguing language will be revealed to provide deeper knowledge and clearer perception to unlock the significance the Book of Exodus is explaining to us.

Decoding Dreams

In "Decoding Dreams" international author O.M. Kelly (Omni), introduces a metaphysical interpretation of the dreams we dream. At times, we may believe that dreams allow us to peer into another world. O.M. Kelly provides the codes for us to understand that other world of dreams—or, through the Shamanic Principles, our "Vision Worlds". Dreams are created through your unconscious/higher mind communicating back to you; dreams are reminding you of the lessons that you need to understand regarding yourself. You cannot hear them if your mind is filled with incessant chatter. The ego refuses to conform when it is in control of the moment. Dreams can range from a pleasant dream, which could be a recommendation to add to what you are doing, to a nightmare, which is a wake-up call from your higher self regarding what you are doing to yourself. As you read this book, keep in mind that learning to metaphysically interpret your dreams is a step-by-step process. Areas covered in the book are: Dream Representations (Animal Kingdom and the Human Kingdom), Questions and Answers about Dreams, and Dream Interpretations.

Reprint coming in the near future.

www.ingramcontent.com/pod-product-compliance
Lightning Source LLC
Chambersburg PA
CBHW051537010526
44107CB00064B/2753